A 'Shore … e

Rich Pickings … y
on the Sea an… …the Sea Shore

To the loved, Claire
(and Isaac) with my
compliments & sincere best wishes
from Swasie
x!

Swasie Turner MBE

Published by D&M Heritage Press
on behalf of Swasie Turner

First published 2017

ISBN: 978-1-911148-11-1

Contents

Preface

The author brings to life in his *pictures n' scriptures* the life that abounds on the sandy beaches and inshore waters of our coastline. From early childhood he acquired an addiction of exploring and learning all about the organisms and creatures from seaweed to jellyfish and also shells, seabirds and insects that inhabit the sands and gullies. Even as a child he became an ardent gatherer of edible shellfish and crustaceans and became a keen sea 'fisherman' to satisfy what became an insatiable appetite for seafood in general. As Swasie grew into adulthood he had by now made many friends in the fishing fraternity. Eventually he was to purchase his own fishing boat to indulge his passion out among them in our coastal waters. As he had been introduced so young to the wonders of our shores, he too introduced and encouraged his own son Ron and daughter Jo from early childhood to enjoy all that prevailed on our shores. Like their father, they too soon 'got the taste'! and accompanied him whenever they could. Even though Swasie was not a *professional* fisherman, he was certainly a very keen amateur that enjoyed sea fishing as a hobby. Most unusual was that even being a 'copper' didn't prevent him being accepted as *'one of them'* amongst the hardy and tough ranks of the local fishermen and shrimpers. This book is an 'education' to those unfamiliar with what goes on in the sea and about our shores and as you go through the pages, the smell of the salty shore and the benefits of abundant fresh air will be sure to fill your nostrils!

Foreword

By Former RNLI Lifeboat Coxswain David Dodd MBE

David Dodd MBE

As I have known Swasie for (*many*) decades I found his book's '*adventures*' and reminiscences very interesting. Having come from generations of a 'Lifeboat' family I have spent many, many enjoyable (and sometimes not so enjoyable!) years both on the sea *shore* and on the sea itself. Many times, Swasie and I have 'shared' the same lumpy waters out fishing and shrimping in the Dee estuary and Irish Sea off Wirral's coastline. Like me, Swasie has also been actively shrimping, cockling and fishing since *his* own early childhood.

He eventually became a police officer but still maintained his 'nautical' hobby when off duty and eventually he too became a *fishing boat* owner. Being a professional fisherman and local (Hoylake) lifeboat crewman (eventually being promoted to the privileged height of the Lifeboat's Coxswain) I can recall Swasie having assisted in an occasional 'rescue' of people who became cut off by the tide, or assisting those whose boats had broken down. In one case he towed a fellow fisherman whose nets had become entangled in the boat's propeller, many miles back from sea to the safety of his moorings where the problem was safely sorted out. I also remember a particularly sad occasion when we both had to professionally *join forces* when he was a police sergeant at Wallasey and I joined him in my RNLI role at Moreton embankment to sadly recover the body of a sea angler who had, days earlier been reported missing at sea. The book's many illustrations (and amusing cartoons) adequately portray to those readers who are 'landlubbers' that fishing (even as a hobby) is not an easy life, especially during inclement weather. Nevertheless they do give an adequate insight into where *and how* our cockles are harvested and fish dinners and shrimp cocktails are caught and brought ashore to the table. Although, Swasie's police career (and inshore boating activities) were sadly brought to a premature end due to him being seriously injured on duty, he nevertheless managed to pick himself up and adapt to a new way of life on the seat of his pants in a wheelchair. He became an ardent and successful fundraiser for numerous worthy charities which he enthusiastically continues with to this day. This book is a very entertaining read for all ages to enjoy and I strongly recommend Swasie's very enlightening, informative and sometimes amusing anecdotal book to all.

David Dodd MBE

Chapter One

Learning the Wonders (and Dangers) of Nature

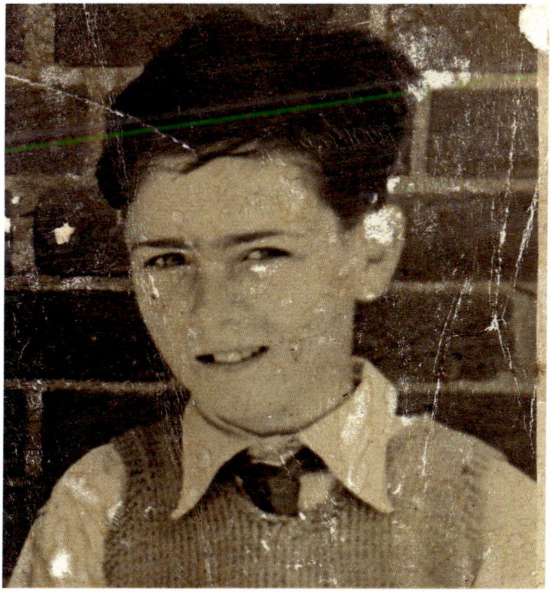

The young author soon became an enthusiastic 'beachcomber'

Being blessed with having been born *almost* on the nearby beaches of our Wirral coastline, almost as soon as I could walk, I was down on the shore accompanying my parents as they picked cockles and winkles for us to enhance our 'gastronomic delights'. By the time I was four years old I had learned to swim. My swimming and diving skills were then honed at the open air scouts baths, secreted in the woods near my home where scouts and guides from all over the country held their annual camps.

Author about to 'take the plunge' into the Scouts baths

Even during the winter, when the pool was not in use my pal Arthur (Archie) Royle (who remains a very close friend to this day) and I would climb over the fence to swim in the dark green, frog infested waters come what may! By the time I was five years old we had become the proverbial '*fish taken to the water*' as Arthur and I continually utilised the facilities at the scouts' baths whether they were open or not. Once we could swim, we also couldn't resist taking every opportunity to get down to the nearby shore with either of our parents so we could enjoy swimming in the sea. It was then, that my love affair with the shore and its environments took a hold.

I soon became acutely interested in all that went on amongst the rocks and rock pools. From the moment I toddled onto the beach, my parents made sure I would become familiar with those creatures that were dangerous, poisonous or harmful. Such aquatic little demons include the *deadly poisonous* Weever fish, (whose excruciatingly painful sting can even prove fatal in some cases), crabs that give painful nips and stinging jellyfish that abounded out and about in the pools or lay on top of, or buried beneath, the sand. Due to such dangers I *strongly* advocate that adequate, protective footwear should always be worn on the beach when venturing out *beyond* the high water line. The 'Tide line' is never in the same place at the same time two days following. It varies from day to day, and according to where you are, may be rising higher, or falling back. The tidal movement forms a rhythm which is controlled by the gravitational pull of the moon. On the side of the earth nearest to the moon there is a greater pull on the water, thus causing a high tide. Since the earth rotates once every 24 hours there are two tides every 24 hours. Due to the moon circling the earth the time between high and low water is roughly six and a quarter hours so each day the times of the high tides vary by about one hour.

At the time of a new moon and full moon, the sun, earth and moon are in a straight line so there is an even greater gravitational pull. This causes the sea to rise very high up the shore then recede a long way out. These big tides are called 'Spring Tides'. After the new and full moon the tides dwindle until, a week later, the tides move only a short distance up and down the shore. These are called 'Neap Tides'.

The movement of the tides is a big factor regarding where plants and creatures live on the shore because the amount of time they are under water varies with the tide. Before venturing out onto the shore, for safety reasons, it is vitally important to be aware of the times and heights of the tides and it would be advisable and beneficial to purchase a 'Tide Table' which are widely available in the numerous newsagents, harbour masters, yachting stores ships chandlers, and fishing tackle and sports shops. When venturing out near the low water line, it is *absolutely essential* to be fully aware of the time when the tide will turn and start to flood. When fishing with a hand net be *very* wary in case you net a weever fish!

My father went to great lengths to educate me about the dangers that lurked and I was religiously taught what were *the 'Good, the Bad and the Ugly'* down on the shore's sandy wastes. Eventually I was able to distinguish which creatures and fish were edible *and which were not.* I became 'addicted'

DEADLY – Lesser Weever fish lies half buried in the sand

to savouring the delights of those that would satisfy what would become my lifelong insatiable seafood and shellfish appetite. My enthusiasm knew no bounds and I relished my regular outings down to the shore where I would *optimistically* paddle into the shallow waters' edge hoping my little hand net would scoop a monster cod while dad was busy cockling nearby!

The Common Cockle is also known as the Edible Cockle. It is a 'bivalve' mollusc which means it has a soft body enclosed inside its shell. Common Cockles can be found in sandy bays and estuaries all around England. They bury themselves under the sand when they are not feeding or when the tide is out. The shells are strong and thick and the outer shell is off white in colour. Common Cockles release their eggs in water where they develop and hatch and settle on sandy sea beds to develop into adult Common Cockles.

Estuaries provide habitats for a large number of organisms and support a very high productivity and provide habitats for many fish nurseries such as salmon and sea trout. Also, migratory bird populations make use of estuaries. Many species of fish and invertebrates have various methods of control or conform to the shifts in salt concentrations; many animals also burrow to avoid predation. Sadly some estuaries are under threat from human activities such as pollution and overfishing. They can also be threatened by sewage, coastal settlement, land clearance and possible events far upstream as industrial, agricultural and domestic waste enter rivers and are discharged into estuaries. Contaminants are also introduced which do not disintegrate rapidly in the marine environment such as plastics, pesticides and various metals.

In the sandier parts of many estuaries are cockle beds, areas where the common cockle lives in vast numbers, often exceeding 1000 per square yard. They feed through their syphons, drawing in plant debris, microscopic plants and a few very small animals such as larval crabs. Unlike some other molluscs, cockles are either male or female. Cockles grow throughout the year but growth is slower in winter and at this time the edge of the shell grows thicker and forms a new ring each winter. By counting these rings the age of the cockle can be estimated. Cockles do have enemies such as flounders, plaice, shore crabs and starfish which eat the small ones and the bigger cockles are eaten by Gulls and oystercatchers who hammer them open with their beak.

Cockles are common and plentiful on most areas of the shore and generally live below the tide levels. The cockle is actually quite a gymnast. If it is stranded on the beach or attacked by a predator it can amazingly somersault away by extending its long, orange 'foot', pressing the tip into the sand and thrusting its body over in an arc. The common cockle has growth rings that run around the shell which will give an approximate age of the shell. Some cockle shells have one or more deeply ridged rings which indicate that the cockle has undergone some sort of disturbance such as being washed out of the sand by a storm; this is known as a disturbance ring.

Cockles are easily gathered or harvested from the beach and their presence is many times indicated by them squirting little lets of water from their shells when they are partly submerged in the wet sand. When fished commercially the method of harvesting them is by raking large numbers together then placing them into a riddle to wash away the sand and grit before placing them into sacks. These shellfish are a very popular and a much sought after food commodity to be sold by fish shops throughout the land. They are easy to cook and take little preparation to serve. After washing and placing into

The common (edible) cockle

Hoylake Triggs family fishermen bagging their cockle 'crop'

The end result – A Gastronomic delight

a pan with just a little water the cockle is cooked by being boiled until the shell opens and is easily detached. The tasty morsel is then served with a sprinkling of vinegar to enhance its taste when served with a salad or when accompanying an aperitif.

It is not only the cockle that is a table temptation as there are other, equally delightful shelled 'cuisine' that abound in abundance on our shores. For instance, the many times inconspicuous little Periwinkle is an equally tasty addition to the mouth watering shellfish menu. It can be found attached to the rocks, stones and various structures which will be covered by the tides. It is easily picked and like the cockle, takes little effort or skill to prepare with regard to cooking for consumption.

The common periwinkle or winkle is a small edible sea snail, a mollusc that has gills and an operculum (a lid like flap) across its opening. It is a robust intertidal snail with a dark shell which is ovate, thick and pointed and is a greyish brown in colour. The common periwinkle is mainly found on rocky shores in the higher and middle tidal areas. It sometimes lives in small tidal pools and muddy habitats of estuaries. When climbing, if exposed to

The tasty little Periwinkle

Periwinkles attached to rocks

extreme heat or extreme cold it will withdraw into its shell and start rolling, hoping to hit the water. It mainly grazes on algae, but it will feed on small invertebrates such as the larvae of barnacles when it uses its radula (a row of sharp teeth like protrusions) to scrape algae from the rocks. The winkle reproduces annually shedding its egg capsules directly into the sea. It can also act as a host for various parasites but its growth rate is primarily affected on availability of food and time available for feeding, and not parasites.

Periwinkles are usually found congregating together on small stones or rocks on the middle shore. Sometimes their numbers are very high and winkle gatherers will go to harvest them. In spite of a lot of predation the edible periwinkle is very common and this is because of its highly successful survival techniques. In rough weather it withdraws into its shell and simply 'shuts its door' (closes its flap) and simply allows itself to be rolled about among the waves. When it is exposed by an ebb tide the edible periwinkle produces a mucus which spreads over the rock to enable the shell to 'glue' itself to the rock surface. Rock pools can be a hive of activity which houses many different animals. If you want to discover all the different creatures in the pool you will have to remain still and watch quietly. Every few minutes something will be moving over the bottom of the pool, perhaps a small green shore crab will dart out from one hiding place to another. A prawn may be seen moving over the sand, stopping here and there to examine a food possibility. In and around most pools will be hundreds of barnacles. These are crustaceans related to the crab family. They settle out of the plankton and cement themselves to the rock surface. When the tide comes in and covers them each one will stick out a net-like foot which scoops through the water to catch drifting particles of food. Each one is both male and female and will release its young into the sea. After a while, these larvae will then settle onto the rocks and grow into adult barnacles.

Other permanent residents of our shores are the crab family. There are many different species of crab that inhabit our shore, each with its own way of life; Green shore crabs are a common sight. Like all crabs, the Green shore crab grows by casting away its old shell which takes about 2 to 4 hours to shed. However, for the next two weeks the animal is so defenceless it must hide away until it grows a new, hard shell. A Green shore crab is a multi- purpose crab, hardy and possessing a variety of survival techniques. It frequently hides away in narrow crevices and is equally at home under rocks. It can stay among seaweed where it shelters against 'anchored' vegetation. In rock pools it burrows into the sand to avoid predators.

The most ferocious of all crabs to be found on the shore is the Velvet Swimming Crab. It is a red brown colour and its reaction to threat or disturbance is to sit back and lift its nipper claws, snapping them rapidly as a warning to keep clear. Their rear legs are like paddles; their flattened ends enable them to swim rapidly through the water. Crabs are either male (cock) or female (hen). Their sex can be ascertained by turning over the crab and looking at its 'purse' which is a turned in tail flap at its rear end. A narrow *triangular* purse is that of a male, the broader based triangular purse is that of a female.

Velvet Swimming Crab

Chapter Two

Coastal and Shoreline 'Rewards' Abound

By the time I entered my teens I had saved a few pounds, shillings and pence as money was in those days via my 'paper round'. I delivered papers for the princely sum of 10/6 (ten shillings and sixpence) per week which equates to *52 and a half pence* in today's decimal currency! During those days, my newsagent shop's owner (Pop Evans) supplied the carrier bike, front and rear lights as well as batteries (which he would renew when required). There was not the dreaded and ridiculous 'Elf n Safety' or 'Jobsworths' as there are today, blighting normal, intelligent common sense and initiative. In days gone by common sense prevailed without the idiotic, politically correct supervision that exists today. My other paper boy pals and I were up and at Pop Evans's shop at 5-30 am awaiting the papers. After we finished our rounds we were

'POP' Evans's paper shop in the distance with sun blind down.

able to snatch an hour's sleep before getting up and ready for school. At the end of the day after school, we would then deliver the 'Liverpool Echo' evening newspaper before then getting home for our evening meal. Oh what *wonderful* everlasting memories of those distant days are? After giving my parents the majority of my 'wages', I managed to save money for the bits and pieces I needed for foraging on the shore in the form of nets, rakes, buckets and riddles etc , *all* courtesy of my paper round 'wages'!

I started to become quite an ardent and keen visitor to the shore to gather whatever was abundant whether it is shellfish or wet fish. I had made my own shrimp net by fitting a triangular net with a 'cod end' to a piece of strong timber which was then secured to a long pole by a steel bolt and butterfly nut. I had a sack with a looped length of line attached which I would place round my neck and shoulders. The other items of my shrimping (hand netting) gear was at first a 'threepenny' riddle which was also attached to a line around my neck. As time went on and I became more proficient and experienced at shrimping, I increased this to a '*Fourpenny*' riddle. The terms *threepenny* and '*fourpenny*' referred to the mesh size of the riddle, i.e. *three* old *(£ s p) pennies placed side by side* was a smaller gauge mesh to that of *four* old pennies side by side. Thus, when riddling shrimps, the '*fourpenny*' riddle would ensure only the larger shrimps would remain inside the riddle allowing the smaller fry to escape and mature. Regular shrimp outings were usually beneficial, even if only a small amount of shrimps were caught. On a good day, catches were quite substantial. However, as one of the regular fishermen once told me, you just *never* know what will be in the net when you lift it out of the water to examine your catch? His words remain with me, it is true, sometimes I would net nothing but weed and debris but other times occupants of my shrimp net would include shrimps, occasionally a prawn or two, crabs and also the vicious Weever fish and perhaps the bonus of a small plaice or round fish big enough for the table. However, I always remain very careful when delving into the net to retrieve the contents to place into my '*fourpenny*' riddle to sort out the 'wheat from the chaff' before emptying the catch it into my sack!

After accompanying one or two fishermen out shrimping on numerous occasions, I learned quickly from them before starting to shrimp solo in my

You never know what *ends up in the net!*

early teens. This hobby would continue on throughout the whole my working life. I eventually became part of the area's enthusiastic and hardy regulars who fished, cockled and shrimped the local shoreline no matter what time of the day or night. I purchased a head torch to add to my nocturnal shrimping resources as a hand torch was awkward to use when netting, riddling or bagging the catch. Another extremely essential piece of equipment I considered to be most important was the pocket compass which would eventually, and dramatically, 'come into its own' to totally justify its existence.

One autumn afternoon during a perfectly 'normal' day I ventured out towards the distant low water line for a day's hand netting for shrimps. As I made my way over the sands to the sea I was joined by two other men I knew by sight as they too made their way out to fish for shrimps. Although one carried a shrimp net over his shoulder and the other carried a riddle and sack, both, in my opinion, were not suitably 'attired' for a shrimping 'expedition' as they were dressed in casual clothing. Like me one carried the

A 'shore' *essential item to have at hand*

net and wore waders but he only wore a flimsy T shirt (whereas I wore a thicker garment for insulation should the temperature drop). His pal carried a riddle and sack, but *he* too was wearing inadequate protection, just a cotton shirt, jeans and *trainers*, out there on the shore among the elements? Neither wore waterproof clothing should the weather become inclement. As we made our way along '*Waders* man' spotted my compass which was clipped to the braces of my waders. He cynically remarked that I was being 'a bit over the top' and asked me why the hell I needed a compass when I was only walking a couple of miles across the sand *in broad daylight.* '*Trainers* man' then sarcastically joined in and quipped by asking if I was *going on a 'Safari'*? Both were amused by my having a compass just to go onto the shore. However, what I hoped I would *never* experience did in fact occur. A totally unexpected crisis suddenly occurred 'out of nowhere' with an absolute vengeance on that day! Such a scenario that would not only amaze and remain with me forever, but would make the two inexperienced and cocky 'fishermen' eat their words – *and how*!!

My compass was to prove invaluable and *well and truly* earned its keep on that day. Without doubt, it *saved the three of us* from a potential, *almost certain* life threatening disaster. At first, all was well as '*Waders* man' and I entered the water up to our waists for a hopeful harvest of shrimps. Meanwhile '*Trainers* man' optimistically stayed on the wet sand with the riddle and sack to sift and bag his pal's (potential) catch. On this day the tide was *very* far out as it was a 'spring tide' and we were shrimping about two miles offshore. Normally in similar circumstances, when the tide turned I would continue to push my net until a quarter of an hour or so into the start of the flood which was adequate time to enable me to leave the water, riddle my catch, bag the shrimps then take the long walk back to the embankment. However, on this *normal* day conditions were to radically and almost instantly change! All of a sudden, within five short minutes, a sea mist descended and *totally* enveloped everywhere with a thick 'pea soup' fog which reduced visibility to no more than five yards. In no time I lost sight of my two fellow shrimpers. Apart from the sound of the waves gently lapping on the sand nearby everywhere became silent. The tide then turned and started to make its way in. The two individuals *somewhere* nearby, started to panic and each shouted and asked where each other was. It was a horrendous and most frightening scenario which I had *never* experienced before on the shore. Visibility went quickly down to zero. Eventually (and luckily) I managed to locate the other two and together *with the aid of my compass*, we made our way slowly back to the shore with the tide virtually 'snapping at our heels'!

It was due *entirely* to enlisting the aid of my compass that we were able to 'navigate' our way back to the safety of the shoreline. Not only did my fellow shrimpers learn the folly of their careless and dangerously naive behaviour on that day, I too was profusely grateful to the little 'life saver' that I always carried securely clipped to me, as without such an important piece of kit, the three of us would have quickly become totally disorientated. I am *convinced* we would not have survived and made it back to the distant shore to safety. This was indeed a prime example of the importance of having such a vitally important instrument with you *at all times* when venturing far out offshore and into the water at low tide. Although I continued to see the 'dynamic duo' now and again here and there, I *never* saw either of those two overconfident and totally out of touch (safety wise) shrimp 'fishermen' out on the shore again after their near miss and lucky escape. Had I not been there on that day with my inconspicuous but all important compass, the consequences of *their* folly do not bear thinking about!

The different species of edible shellfish on our shores are truly amazing. As time went on my curiosity as to what was this and what was that made me almost a connoisseur. As well as spending the day cockling, shrimping or picking periwinkles, another rewarding aspect of 'shoreline' cuisine was the tasty razor fish. Its long, narrow shell is quite unmistakable as it resembles that of a closed 'cut throat' razor. The mollusc is a fantastically fast burrower and can burrow down deeply into the sand actually faster than anyone can dig, so fast are they that their speed of descent can reach up to *18 inches per second.*

When out seeking this desirable gastronomic delight, the first thing to do is find its signs. The best time to do this is on a day with a low (*Spring*) tide and walk slowly *backwards* along the sand. Keep a sharp eye on the sand between your feet and if a razor is there, it will propel a sudden jet of water into the air. As it subsides, a hole will appear in the sand which will open rapidly as the water left in it drains away. A well tried and tested method to catch the elusive clam is to then pour salt into the hole. The razor shell will then pop up a couple of inches and can be quickly grabbed and pulled from the sand. The clam shell, lying an inch or so under the sand feels the vibration of your feet and immediately burrows downwards; the jet of water is the result of its sudden reaction. It pushes its long foot (similar to that of the cockle) out from the lower end of its shell, down through the sand and pumps it full of blood to get a grip. It repeats this quickly so the razor shell dives down in a series of jerks. It would be far too fast to dig a razor shell out as there's no simple trick other than the method I have described. To become proficient at catching the fast razor shellfish nothing less than practice and patience is the secret of success. However, the end result is well worth the effort, and, like the cockle, periwinkle and others, the razor fish is an excellent addition to a seafood meal.

Freshly pulled Razor shell Fish

Cooking the Razor Fish

As a tempting gastronomic treat, try the following for a delicious feast for four

Chilli and Garlic Razor Fish with Saffron Mayonnaise

For this you will need the following ingredients.

For the mayonnaise

A pinch of saffron

2 teaspoons of boiled water

1 teaspoon of Harissa

Three and a half ounces (100g) of mayonnaise

For the breadcrumbs, 1 tablespoon of olive oil, 2 ounces (50g) crusty bread, torn into small pieces. Small bunch of parsley roughly chopped.

12 fresh, live razor fish. Discard any that do not open when tapped sharply or any that are damaged or have cracked shells. 7 fl ounces (200ml) of olive oil. 1 red chilli finely chopped and 8 garlic cloves, finely chopped.

Method

- For the saffron mayonnaise, mix the saffron and hot water together and set aside for 15 minutes.
- Mix the harissa, mayonnaise and saffron in a bowl, cover with cling film and set aside.
- For the breadcrumbs, heat the oil in a small frying pan and cook the breadcrumbs for 3-4 minutes. Stir constantly until the crumbs are golden brown and crisp. Stir in the parsley and set aside to cool.
- Cook the razor fish in a pan of boiling water for *FIVE TO TEN SECONDS* or until the shells open. Drain immediately and discard any that fail to open.
- Heat the oil over a low heat in a small saucepan and add the garlic, chilli, salt and lots of freshly ground black pepper. Cook for ten minutes, stirring constantly then remove the pan from the heat.
- When the razor fish are cool enough, carefully ease the razor fish out of its shell and using a sharp knife separate the two sides of the shell. Cut out the brown sack which runs along the length of each clam and discard. Trim off the dark tipped end and pull away the long feathery

gills. Wipe away any sandy bits. Snip the fish diagonally with scissors and return the pieces to one half of the shell.

- Preheat the grill to high. Arrange the clams in a large, oven proof dish. Reheat the oil until warm then gently pour over the clams. Place them under the grill and cook for 2-3 minutes.
- Scatter the breadcrumbs over and serve with the saffron mayonnaise.

The exciting meal is ready to serve.

Having mentioned some of the edible delights that can be gathered from our shores, there is another shellfish that is equally popular at the table, the mussel. These little treasures anchor themselves by little threads to rocks, breakwaters or any object that is at hand for them to secure themselves to. They feed by drawing in seawater and filtering out thousands of tiny floating particles. Apart from the mussels I obtain from areas on the shore, most of the mussels we eat are now are bought from the fishmonger. These are mainly cultivated on ropes suspended from floats in clean waters. These plump up naturally on plankton. On the plate they are very satisfying and can be relied upon to bring flavour to the table.

'My' shoreline shell fishing grounds at Moreton have a unique history which, although I digress slightly, I think is worthy of inclusion. In 1962 British United Airways set up an experimental Hovercraft service between Moreton and Rhyl. This was to be the first such hovercraft passenger service in the world. At the Moreton end the craft would come to a stop on the sand to allow its passengers to board or disembark as the case may be. Occasionally it would come to a standstill on the slanting concrete embankment itself.
Prior to the Hovercraft service the promenade (or Moreton embankment) would only see walkers etc as they wandered each way along towards New Brighton or Hoylake in the opposite direction. However, during the (short) period of service the area at the Moreton 'terminus' would be crowded with onlookers and enthusiasts (which many times included myself) and keen photographers. The service also brought a few pennies to the local little tea stalls on the other side of the embankment to enhance their takings considerably.

Since the service ended the activities dwindled and now only one snack stall survives but the little stall is a very prosperous fish and chip bar which is blessed with regular and numerous customers who travel to the venue to

Busy tea and snack stalls the other side of the embankments at Moreton

On the seaward side, the Hovercraft awaits its passengers for Rhyl

enjoy its gastronomic delights. Two of those regular enthusiastic customers include my daughter Jo (Cocklelily) and myself on as many occasions as we can get to the little 'chippy'.

Same venue now, shows Jo (Cocklelily) bringing chips for her and dad to enjoy

And now, to resume and get back to furnishing tasty recipes for all to enjoy...

Mussels have the most impressive nutritional profile of all shellfish. Mussels are also a brilliant source of vitamins. When eating mussels, always ensure that they are first *de bearded* (i.e. the 'hair' is removed from the centre of the flesh). This is a dark hair like protrusion from the core of the 'meat' and is easy to spot and remove.

Mussels attached to rocks

Cooked and ready to eat

Here is an excellent recipe for a great, quick (mussels) supper for four. Always make sure shells are clean as they will be wallowing around in the stew.

Mussel Supper

2 tbsp olive oil
20 g butter
2 red onions, peeled and finely chopped
1 small chilli, deseeded and finely chopped.
A pinch of salt
3 garlic cloves, crushed
A few shreds of saffron
A head of fennel, trimmed and finely sliced
3 large red potatoes, peeled and cut into small chunks
800 ml fish stock
Peel and juice of half an orange
1 bay leaf
1 kg mussels, shells cleaned and 'debearded' (Hair removed)
250 ml white wine
Small handful of parsley, chopped.

- Heat half the oil and butter in a large pan and add the onions and chilli. Reduce the heat, add a small pinch of salt and cook for 10 minutes
- Add the garlic, saffron and fennel, turn up the heat and cook for a couple of minutes stirring constantly to prevent the garlic going brown, then add potatoes and fish stock
- Take a small strip of peel from the orange, add to the stew then squeeze in the juice. Add the bay leaf and simmer for fifteen minutes until the potatoes are just cooked.
- Stir gently for a minute or so then leave to simmer on a low heat.
- Heat the remaining oil in a saucepan and add the mussels. Stir for two minutes, add the wine, put the lid on and leave until the mussels open wide.

- Transfer the mussels to the stew but discard empty shells and any shells that haven't opened then pass the liquid from the pan into the stew through a fine sieve.
- Add the parsley and season to taste. Serve with a salad of grated carrot and spring onions with a thick slice of bread.

Although there are many more shellfish out there for the table, which will be featured in the later pages, (including more appropriate and appetising recipes) now we come to the very varied selection of *wet* fish. These can be caught by various means and the fish can be divided into three main categories. Round sea fish are by far the largest group which include cod, mackerel and mullet. These fish can be very small like whitebait or huge, like sharks. The next category is 'flat' fish that swim on their sides such as skate, dabs plaice and halibut. These are easy identifiable because of their distinctive colouring. They are dark on one side, (the upper side) to assist camouflage and white on the lower side. Another unusual feature is they also have unusual positioning of the eyes which are both on the same (upper), dark side of the head. The last group is freshwater fish which include pike and salmon. All of these are born in rivers or lakes, however, some of them, such as salmon, spend all of their adult lives in the ocean only returning to the river where they were born, to spawn. It is widely known that fish are good for you as it has a low fat content and contains many nutrients such as iron, B vitamins, fluorine and sometimes calcium. Fish can be caught by various means. First, the rod and line with baited hook. This method of fishing is the *main* facility and hobby of those of the amateur fishing fraternity from children to adults as well as highly professional anglers. Angling is a very popular hobby worldwide and needs no explaining. The hobby has many times been kindled and starts in early childhood with a stick and length of string with a worm tied on the end with the proverbial jam jar to house the catch of *Jacksharps, sticklebacks, tiddlers or tadpoles.* No doubt each and every one of us has also been along that road during our childhood at one time or another?

To many who became 'hooked' (forgive the pun!) on this pastime, this has then gone on to manifest itself by the purchasing of a (sometimes) expensive

A young enthusiast's jar full of 'Taddies' from the pond

rod and reel. There are two types of vehemently keen rod and line fishermen; the first is the 'coarse' fisherman. He fishes the fresh waters of ponds, lakes and estuaries for the *sole* (again, forgive the pun) pleasure of seeing and identifying whatever fish he catches before returning the fish back into the depths. Sometimes there are venues which are 'out of bounds' and fishing some ponds and lakes are forbidden for one reason or another.

There are some places that do not permit fishing

Chapter Three

A Wider Selection and Broader Spectrum of Fishing

The enthusiastic and ardent angler will many times record or photograph his catch with pride for posterity before returning it to the water. Other times he or she will fish in competitions, again returning the catch after weighing and recording whatever has been caught. The other, equally keen rod and line fisherman is the sea (or boat) angler. Sometimes the sea angler will catch, record and photograph the fish too before returning it to the depths to fight another day. However, the sea or boat fisherman will also prefer many times retain his catch for the pot. The variety of fish that can be taken from the sea is almost endless, as are the methods of catching them. Worldwide, there are more than 30,000 different species ranging in shape, size and colour.

Again, a popular method is via a sturdy and strong fishing rod which will many times give the fisherman a tough and invigorating fight. Some varieties are easy to catch, such as the Mackerel, while others are extremely hard to land and this is where each participant (fish and human) will each pit their skills during the ensuring 'battle' down in the murky depths!

Mackerel is one of our favourite oily fish and it tastes great griddled, baked, smoked or in a pate.

Regarding the creation of diverse mackerel dishes, any budding, versatile chef can easily utilise his or her skills to furnish a million and one menus as the mackerel is easily obtainable either via the rod or purchasing from the local fishmonger. Here are but a few examples of how easy it is to create an excellent meal of mackerel for the table.

Once the griddle is hot, add the mackerel skin side down. Sprinkle with a pinch of salt and pepper and grate over the zest of a lemon, reduce the heat then cook for a total of eight minutes. Allow to cool then it's ready to eat and as the fish is packed full of Omega 3 the oily fish is full of flavour and is great

Hooking Mackerel, an easy catch

A quartet of fresh Mackerel ready for preparing

added to any form of a salad dish. Another tasty dish is when Grilled, with a marinade of soy, lime and ginger (below). Heat grill and put mackerel, skin side up on a sheet of foil. Grill for 5 minutes then turn over and baste with the marinade and grill for further 5 minutes. This method is excellent served with boiled rice.

Spicy Grilled Mackerel with Fennel Coleslaw

Ingredients:

150g of fat free yogurt
3 teaspoons of creamed horseradish
1 fennel bulb, halved and thinly sliced
1 green apple, cored and halved and thinly sliced
1 grated medium carrot
1 stick of celery and its leaves, finely sliced
A quarter teaspoon of ground cumin
A quarter teaspoon of ground coriander
4 fresh mackerel fillets, boned.
Then serve with 2 tablespoons of roughly torn coriander leaves

Another illustrated example of a quick, easy mackerel meal

Other fish are more difficult to hook and bring aboard, such as the ray family. Rays are distinguished by their flattened bodies and enlarged pectoral fins which are fused to their heads and their gill slits are placed on their ventral surfaces. Rays and skates bodies are designed for living and feeding on the seabed. The species of ray most targeted by local (British) anglers are the common skate and the thornback ray (also known as Roker).

The common skate is the largest species of skate in the world and can be one of the largest species in British waters. Skate and Rays are closely related to sharks as they share common features such as having a skeleton of cartilage. They both feed on crustaceans and molluscs but will also feed on fish such as dabs and flounders. Skate populations have been decimated around the country to such an extent that its reduced numbers have become so serious in the UK that skate populations are restricted to isolated areas. It is generally boat anglers who target skate as the fish, being so strong and powerful, need to be slowly pumped up from the seabed to the surface when it can then be gaffed and brought aboard. However, to catch such a fish from the *shore* would be a *major coup* for an angler and quite a rare achievement. Best baits for enticing ray are mackerel but strips of herring or flatfish can also be used.

Common Skate, a very worthy opponent for the angler

The other highly sought ray fish for the boat angler is the Thornback ray or 'Roker'. This ray too feeds mainly on crustaceans and crabs and will also eat flatfish. Always use caution when de hooking either of these two as both have strong and powerful jaws; I strongly advise the use of pliers or forceps when removing the hook from either of the two. Also, after gaffing and handling the Thornback Ray, gloves or hand protection should be used when bringing the fish aboard as the Roker's thorns can easily pierce skin and clothing.

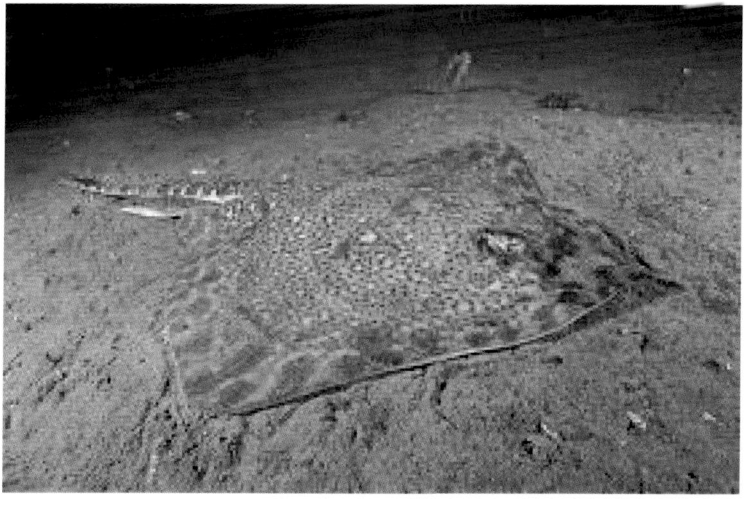

Thornback Ray (or Roker)

Going from such large, strong 'flat fish' as the Skate and Thornback Ray I now turn to those of their smaller cousins such as plaice, flounders and dabs, although ultimately the latter would not demand such physically demanding efforts to land, *all* angling is extremely exciting once the rod bucks and kicks as *anything* could be on the hook once the bait has been taken. When the angler 'strikes' the adrenalin starts to flow. The smaller and more common 'flatties' such as the above three are in abundance in our waters and *all* fish, once they have taken the bait create an exciting and most exhilarating experience whether the angler is fishing from a boat or from the shore.

Skate wings can grace the plates of many delightful recipes and here is one such recipe for two to sit down and enjoy.

Skate Wings with Caper Butter and Olive Mash

Ingredients

Two skate wings

Two ounces of plain flour, seasoned with salt and pepper

One tablespoon of olive oil

Sauce

Six ounces of butter

Four tablespoons of lemon juice

Three tablespoons of washed caper berries

Three tablespoons of washed capers

Two tablespoons of roughly chopped parsley

Olive oil mash – Two large peeled potatoes cut into chunks, Four fluid ounces of olive oil, salt and pepper

Method

- Dip the wings in flour
- Heat a large frying pan until hot and add the butter and oil. When the butter starts to bubble add the skate and fry for three minutes on each side.
- Make the sauce by placing the butter into a small pan over medium heat until the butter is melted and nut brown in colour. Add the lemon juice, caper berries and parsley and stir well.
- For the olive oil mash, place the potatoes in a pan and cover with water. Bring to the simmer and cook for ten to fifteen minutes until tender then drain off. Mash the potatoes then add the olive oil and stir well, season with salt and pepper. Serve by placing skate onto plate then add two spoonfuls of mash and spoon over the caper butter.
- What a treat!

Another method of catching sea fish is via lay lines. Many times during my childhood and teens I accompanied local fishermen out to erect, bait and collect numerous fish from the lines they had placed far out from shore prior to the flood and ebb of the tides.

I never failed to be impressed by the amount of various types of fish we collected. The means of creating this method were simple, although a certain amount of effort was required to bring about the ultimate operation.

The method was to make out to near the low water line then dig a 2 ft hole in the sand into which is placed the willow stake. Once in place replace the wet sand into the hole. The stake will now remain secure, firmly anchored by the bag of sand and nails at its base. Repeat the procedure with the rest of the stakes, placed at 6 yard intervals. To each stake attach a strong length of line onward to join the rest of the planted stakes. The hooks attached to the short lengths of fishing line are then secured to the main line and baited. Once this lengthy operation is completed return to shore and allow the tide to flood and ebb before returning at the next low water to (hopefully) retrieve a 'healthy' catch?

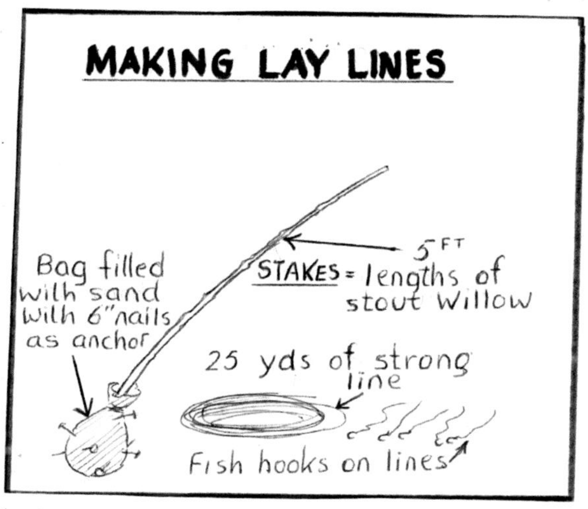

Creating the equipment for Lay Lines

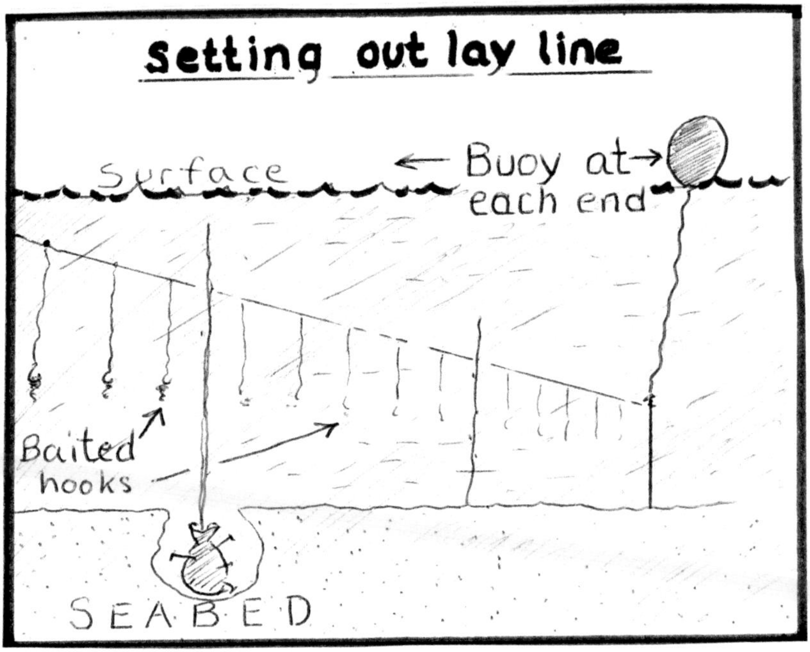

Becoming operational

I have illustrated via my diagrams how I was taught to make and set out baited lay lines at low water. During my early childhood my neighbourhood was blessed with a lot of woodland, open country and the nearby shoreline where wildlife abounded. Living in the locality was a man who was a keen taker of rabbits and wood pigeons for 'the pot' from the local area and its private estates; he was also a knowledgeable, prolific and extremely efficient shore fisherman. Although he was a popular hard working professional, he was jokingly referred to as the local 'poacher' and was indeed a character that enhanced the locality! I was originally his paper delivery boy and once he became aware of my keen interest in fishing he would take me out with him on his various fishing expeditions (day or night), to retrieve fish from the lay lines he had pedantically constructed and securely embedded into the sand out across the beach at the low water mark. Many times I witnessed his labours had been well and truly rewarded and he would fill (and share some of) his sack with the fish retrieved from his homemade lines. This man taught me all I know about the various (and secretive) forms of life on and below the sandy shore and the rewarding and appetising contents of the local waters. I will always remain extremely grateful to him. He and his family became firm and everlasting friends, a friendship that exists to this day as strong as ever. My diagrams illustrate the method I was taught to make and set up lay lines and I have found this method to have remained a total success over the years. The reason that lengths of willow are preferred as stakes are because they are both strong and also flexible so that they don't snap with the weight of any fish caught and still remain strong and upright during tide movement. The small sand filled sacking bag with its protruding long nails secured at the base of each stake ensures an excellent anchorage. To the end and centre stakes a floating marker buoy should be firmly secured to indicate the position of the length of line and stakes beneath the surface. As well as them being able to indicate and identify the position of the line when wading out at the end of the ebb tide, they will also warn any boats in the area to keep clear of an underwater obstruction.

To furnish the angler's or lay line fisherman's hooks will require a tempting bait to entice the fish to bite. Some bait is relatively easy to acquire (or buy) while other more exotic baits are more difficult to come by. Two of the main sea angler's preferences for his hooks are lugworm and rag worm. Both of these tasty (to the fish) specimens are to be found under the sand when the tide has gone out.

Rag worms live burrowed in the sand and mud and vary in colour from brown or bright red. The common rag worm is about four and a half inches in length. Its head has extendable sharp pinchers and the larger species can give a nasty nip. At low tide they can be dug from the beaches and estuaries. When they have been dug out with a fork or spade, wrap each one in a piece of newspaper to preserve until use. Rag worms are best used fresh but they can be safely stored in a fridge for up to 6 days. When baiting a hook with rag worm, thread onto the hook below its head or push the hook into its mouth

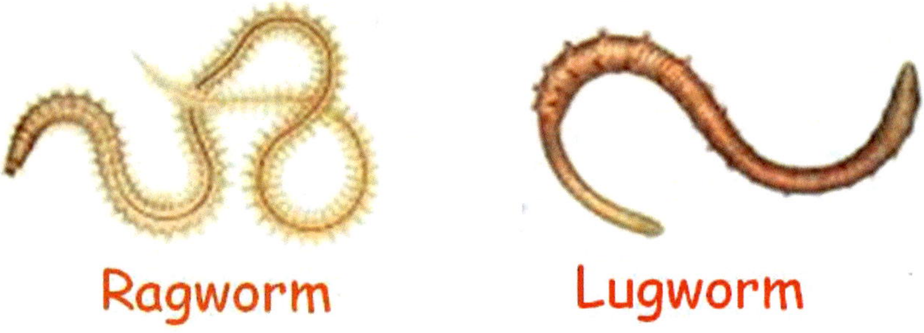

Frequent Baits dug from the beach

Rag worm

and slide the worm along the whole length of the hook's shank. Bring the hook out through the rag worm's side. Long worms can be broken into two halves or many pieces to furnish two or more hooks. The worms are strong and solid and will remain secure on the hooks.

Lugworms also live burrowed about eighteen inches below the sand or mud in 'U' shaped tunnels. They discard their excrement up and out into telltale coils onto the surface. The worms are about 6 inches in length and, like the rag worm, may be dug out at low tide. Again, until used, wrap in clean dry newspaper and keep separate. Lug can also be stored in a fridge but only for up to 3 days after which they should be discarded if not used as they give off an extremely foul and pungent smell when dead or decomposing. When baiting a hook with lug, thread the hook through its head or where the thin tail meets the thicker trunk, some fishermen prefer to remove the tail when fishing to release fish enticing juices.

Lugworm

Chapter Four

Forewarned, Father Neptune's Dangerous Creatures Abound in, and out, *of the Water*

The coastal waters of the Irish Sea contain a number of species of jellyfish, many of which have venomous long tentacles. Anyone unfortunate enough to touch or be brushed by these tentacles could receive a poisonous sting from the barbs on those tentacles. Being stung by one of these creatures can be a very painful experience. DO NOT TOUCH any unknown jellyfish, some stings can be severe. Rumour has it that you should urinate on the sting to neutralise the pain? There *is* an element of truth in this rumour, depending on how acidic the urine is. Acidity of urine depends on diet and most of us don't produce urine that is acidic enough to neutralise a jellyfish sting. A more effective (and less embarrassing) method would be to use vinegar as this will deactivate the stinging cells that may be attached to the skin.

The best form of treatment for anyone who is stung is to gently remove any tentacles that are attached using tweezers or wearing gloves, then flood the area affected with vinegar. Do NOT rub the affected skin as this may cause any tentacles still attached to release more venom. In the absence of vinegar, pour sea water over the area to help reduce the rash. Fresh water would not be of any help as this will in fact cause more irritation. Some examples of jelly fish that swim and float about in our waters are the Barrel, Moon, Compass, Blue and Lion's Mane. I have seen a number of these in our local waters or washed up on the beach. The Lion's Main is easy to identify as it is a very large jellyfish which is dark red or brown in colour with what looks like a lion's mane, hence its name. I advise anyone seeing this unfriendly creature to give it a wide berth, in or out of the water. Jelly fish can still sting if lying on the shore, dead. Another deadly jellyfish that I have seen on rare occasions is the deadly Portuguese Man O'War. This nasty specimen can inflict a deadly and serious sting. I would strongly advise anyone sighting either of these two creatures, especially if they are in large numbers, to inform the Coast Guard immediately. These would be a danger if washed up on the shore and children were to go near or touch them. Treat ALL jellyfish with extreme caution however small and harmless they may appear and avoid swimming in the sea where they appear to be.

We get these jellyfish drifting in from warmer waters most years in the UK. Below are some illustrations of such jellyfish that visit and litter our shores which are *most* unwelcome and dangerous, these unsavoury visitors to be avoided at all costs.

Beware of 'harmless looking' Jellyfish marooned on the beach

The awesome Lion's Head stinging Jellyfish

The Deadly Portuguese Man O'War jellyfish

Such is the venom of the 'Man O'War' illustrated above; a person stung can easily suffer severe shock. The Portuguese Man O'War can kill a small child and even adults who might be suffering from heart conditions. When giving assistance to a casualty who has been stung, beware of the poisonous barbs embedded in the casualty's skin; *always* take extreme care not to get stung yourself by these.

WARNING – Vinegar works on all jellyfish stings *EXCEPT* those inflicted by the Portuguese Man O'War where using vinegar can *worsen* the stings and trigger the release of *more* toxins. For treating stings from this jellyfish use sea water, or sea water and bicarbonate of soda mixed together as a paste. Even better, use *hot* sea water if possible. Do not use fresh water to treat Portuguese Man O'War stings as non salt water can induce the stings to release more toxins into the skin. Do not bandage the stung area as this will have the same result as using fresh water. Fortunately, here on the beaches in the UK such stings from these unsavoury creatures are rare. However, anyone venturing onto the shore below the high water line should always be aware of the danger that exists if such creatures are lying around in the vicinity, especially while swimming or where children are playing or paddling.

Chapter Five

Furnishing Some Examples of Delightful Cuisine

Moving away from such a most avoidable species of the sea to another slippy fish, but this time, another sought after fish, the eel, which originally spawns in the Sargasso Sea in the Western Atlantic. Although there are many variations of eel, the eels I have caught have all been the common (European) eel. This fish is found in streams and brooks and the still waters connected to them. They can sometimes grow up to five feet long and its skin is covered in mucus to protect it from changes in the water's salinity. The eel can breathe through its skin which allows it to survive in water with low oxygen levels.

A number of eels are caught from the sea, especially from beaches that are near to estuaries. Part of the common eel's fascinating life cycle is spent in the sea and part in fresh water rivers. The adults have long, narrow bodies with a continuous anal and dorsal fin. The skin is slimy and the lower jaw

Common (European) eel

Landing a slippery eel

is longer than the upper jaw. Their colour depends on the age of the fish; they are usually brown, black or olive green and have yellowish bellies. Some adults are silver. The eel is a popular and much sought after catch by course anglers and sea fishermen alike, although the majority of the former return their catch to the water, many sea anglers retain theirs for the pot!

The eel is also a much sought after source of food by predators such as gulls and cormorants and is also a tasty meal for a number of species of fish. Amazingly, the eel can survive out of the water for a long time and can even travel overland on a dark, wet night!

The eel is also a popular addition to various menus for the table. I have caught eels over the years which have enhanced various tasty meals. I prefer the traditional dish of 'jellied eels'.

Although I have many times caught eels on a rod and line from a boat, I have never seen any caught on lay lines. I always found the common eel's favourite bait to be rag or lug worm.

The popular and easily prepared dish of 'Jellied eel'

To remove an eel from the hook I prefer using a damp cloth in my hand to ensure a firm grip on the fish as I remove the hook with the other hand. After dispatching the fish, half sever the head and again holding the fish firmly with a damp cloth in one hand take hold of the head and pull down towards the tail to remove the skin in one piece.

To create the mouth watering dish of jellied eels, wash the fish then cut into 2 inch thick steaks. In the meantime, bring to the boil a pan containing just enough water to cover the steaks. Add two tablespoons of salt to the water and when the water is boiling, add the eel steaks and simmer gently for only a couple of minutes.

As well as the popular jellied eel dish above, there are many other equally appetising and exciting mouth watering dishes that can ensue with the addition of eel to the menu.

One such gastronomic delight is ...

Stir Fried Eel with Black Bean Paste and Garlic

For this the following ingredients are required.

One medium sized European (common) eel

1 teaspoon of corn flour

1 teaspoon of garlic, crushed

Half a teaspoon of ginger root, crushed

2 tablespoons of sesame oil

1 tablespoon of black bean paste

A quarter of a teaspoon of chilli flakes, 2 tablespoons of water, 2 tablespoons of sherry wine, 1 teaspoon of soy sauce and a small onion finely diced.

Method

- Cut the eel into one inch pieces and roll in corn flour. Mix the garlic, ginger, sesame oil, black bean paste and chilli flake in a small bowl with two tablespoons of water. Heat a wok or large skillet until very hot then add the mixture, closely followed by the eel pieces and stir for one minute. Add sherry, soy and onion and stir fry for five minutes until eel is cooked.
- Serve with plain steamed rice.

Delicious meal of Stir fried eel and black bean paste with steamed rice

Another simple variation on the eel menu to delight the taste buds for a mid-day snack and one which is quick and easy to prepare, ***Fried Eel***. All you need for this is:

1 eel cut into two inch pieces
1 egg slightly beaten
Quarter of teaspoon of salt
Half a cup of flour
Add pepper
Small amount of fat to fry

Method

- Part boil the eel for 3 minutes then dip into the egg, roll in flour seasoned with salt and pepper to taste.
- Fry for 5 minutes on either side then serve.

Yet another one of the limitless eel recipes. This exciting dish of ***Seared Eel Cutlets*** is for two and is certainly one to please. For this you need

1 cup of flour
1 tablespoon of chopped basil
1 teaspoon of red pepper flake
A pinch of rosemary
1 medium eel, skinned and filleted
4 tablespoons of sunflower oil
3 cloves of garlic, crushed
1 lemon cut into two halves

Method

- Mix the flour, basil, rosemary and red pepper flakes. Slice the eel into 2 inch cutlets then squeeze the lemon halves onto the cutlets. Coat both sides of the cutlets into the flour mixture then set aside.
- Heat the oil in a skillet on medium low heat. Sauté the crushed garlic until soft for about 1 minute. Add the cutlets into the pan and fry for 3 minutes on each side until the coating is crispy and the eel is cooked through. Serve on a bed of boiled rice.

The most delightful dish of seared eel cutlets with boiled rice

We now return once again to flatfish. The four most common flatfish in our British waters are the Plaice, Flounder, Dab and sole. Plaice are identified by having vivid red spots on its dark brown upper side. Another distinguishing feature is its bony ridge behind its eyes. The underside of the plaice is white with an opaque 'herringbone' pattern visible.

The Flounder has a large broad tail and a big head. The flesh of the flounder appears to be more 'flabby' than that of its two cousins.

The easiest way to tell the Dab from its cousins the plaice and flounder is its rough skin. When the Dab is rubbed from its tail towards its head its skin is rough but when it is rubbed from its head towards its tail its skin is smooth. The Dab also has a pronounced bulge above its pectoral fin and its eyes are larger (bulging) in proportion to its head.

FLATFISH are classed as 'Whitefish' and have lean, textured flesh and each species has its own unique flavour. Flatfish make a very popular and appetizing meal. Members of the flatfish family include Plaice, Lemon Sole,

The Plaice, easily identified by its conspicuous red spots

The Flounder

The Dab

Lemon Sole

Dab, Flounder and Dover sole. (Halibut, Turbot, Brill, Skates and Rays also come under the heading of flatfish and they too have lean white flesh but they differ by being cartilaginous).

The flavours of these different fish match the different cooking methods. Generally, the usual method for plaice, sole dab and founder is grilling, pan frying, baking and deep frying as this gives all a good, tasty and enjoyable result. I have found that Dab with lemon and mint potatoes is a most scrumptious and highly enjoyable meal. Regarding the 'versatile' tasting plaice, this is an ideal inclusion of the traditional fish, chips and peas meal. Another equally enjoyable variation of a plaice menu can be plaice with shellfish and wild garlic. Lemon Sole is also most enjoyable as an addition to chips and peas. Another tempting recipe includes lemon sole with leek, shrimps and capers or perhaps lemon sole goujons with mushy peas and sweet potato chips. Lemon sole is actually a flounder and has delicate, sweet white flesh. It is best cooked simply grilled or fried and served with a light sauce.

All the above are an absolute gastronomic delight and each will furnish a most enjoyable and delicious meal.

The lemon sole for instance is renowned for its wonderful flavour.

A fine example of such a very tasty recipe is

Fillets of Sole with Lemon Sauce and Herbs

This is a great delicately sharp little dish that makes an excellent main course for a summer meal. For this, the following ingredients are required.

4 fillets of lemon sole with the dark skin removed.

Plain flour

1 small lemon

3 oz butter

8 tablespoons of chicken stock

6 tablespoons of dry vermouth

2 tablespoons of finely chopped chives

1 tablespoon of finely chopped parsley

A pinch of dried sage

Salt and freshly ground black pepper

Method

- Coat the fillets with flour seasoned with salt and pepper. Cut the lemon in half lengthways and then into very thin slices, removing the pips.
- Heat the butter in a large frying pan until it starts to foam then add the fish and cook over a medium heat for 3 minutes each side until the fish is just cooked through. Remove the fish to a heated serving dish and keep warm.
- Add the stock and vermouth to the juices in the pan, scraping the pan well. Bring to the boil and cook over a high heat until the liquid is reduced to about a third. Add the herbs and lemon slices, season with extra salt and pepper and simmer for three minutes. Arrange the lemon slices on the fish and pour over the sauce from the pan. Serve at once with boiled new potatoes, mashed potatoes or savoury rice. Accompany with spring greens or leeks.
- This is a meal not to be missed.

Chapter Six

Joining the Boating Fraternity

Boat fishing, out and about in the wild blue yonder on the open sea is both very relaxing and highly invigorating. As well as never knowing what can be caught from the secretive depths the boat angler can very often have a tough fight on his hands to bring aboard whatever had taken his bait. Where-ever one fishes from a boat whether it is on a lake, river or the open sea, safety must be paramount at ALL times. Safety equipment including a first aid kit should be on board and at hand instantly in case of emergency. There should be life jackets for each person aboard, signal flares and I strongly advise the sea angler to take the trouble to qualify to possess and use ship to shore radio. Admittedly boat angling can be expensive at the start but safety must come first at all times.

When rules apply regarding fishing they are in force for a purpose. When out boating on lakes, rivers (or ponds) such rules *must* be complied with at all times. I take *all* forms of involvement on the shore or on the water *very* seriously and angling should be a safely enjoyed hobby at all times and any form of legislation should be complied with.

My keen interest in boats materialised after I was invited out with the local fishermen and shrimpers. I learned a lot from watching and eventually helping them during the numerous outings to catch either shellfish or white fish. I went on to help clean and gut the catch, boil and bag the shell fish catch etc.

Eventually I bought my own little boat, which to me as new member of the boating 'fraternity' was intended to be my own *sea* angling boat. Although only small, it was big enough to accommodate myself and on numerous occasions an equally keen sea angling pal, together with our rods and safety gear (and I christened her '*Swasie 1*'). Sometimes we would venture out minus our rods and instead, fish with 'hand lines', which was a frame with a baited (or feathered when fishing for mackerel) line with weight which was dropped

Irresponsible Boat angling can bring instant retribution!

Author's first (sea) fishing boat (note rig in the distance)

over the side. Then began a patient wait for a hopeful catch to materialise?

Although small, my first boat was 'seaworthy' enough to safely take me out during one hot summer in the past to a rig, three miles out from Hoylake into the Irish Sea where I successfully fished and caught various types with my rod or hand line. While the rig remained in situ I visited the site a number of times after meticulously ensuring conditions (and weather) were favourable. As well as my reliable and sturdy Seagull outboard motor, I also carried a set of oars in reserve.

I enjoyed many hours fishing both solo and with friends in my first sturdy little boat, even though it was only small. However, large oak trees from acorns grow and my ambition, and intention, was to eventually have a bigger boat (when finances allowed!).

My enthusiasm for boat fishing was not only confined to my locality. As time went on I started to venture to venues further afield. One of my favourite destinations was the beautiful Welsh seaside village of Abersoch

The offshore rig, 3 miles out from Hoylake

Author's pal fishing with a hand line near to rig

to where I would travel with friends and enjoy a day's deep sea fishing. We would be taken far out to sea aboard a large sea angling boat under the care of the late Brian Jones, a very popular and knowledgeable local skipper. Brian's knowledge and skill always ensured a bountiful catch was obtained by all aboard his vessel, which would accommodate a number of equally enthusiastic (and by the end of the day, satisfied) anglers.

Another equally beautiful venue I enjoyed visiting many times from early on for a day's fishing, (and still do to this day), was the wonderfully scenic island of Anglesey off the North Wales coast. Here too, a successful day's fishing was nearly always guaranteed. I would go out in a friend's boat from the rocky protection of Bull bay to fish offshore where we would be rewarded with various specimens of fish such as whiting, skate, mullet, plaice and even large tope (shark). My pal 'Skippy' Jackson, a resident of Bull Bay, also utilised his skills to furnish me with freshly caught crab and lobster during my visits to his beautiful island paradise.

At the time, although only a young man, 'Skippy' was a prolific and highly skilled local fisherman. Not only was he a knowledgeable sea fisherman and angler, his skills also included the catching of crab and lobster. I never once failed to return home from a day's fishing down at Anglesey without a variety of culinary delights from father Neptune's generous coffers!

The whole of the North Wales coastline area is nothing short of a sea angler's 'Mecca'. As well as furnishing a most enjoyable and rewarding day's fishing, the nearby panoramic delights of Snowdonia and its beautiful mountain range are also a photographer's dream should he or she be an ardent and budding 'David Bailey'. Such is the enticing facilities and beauty of Anglesey (Ynys Mon) that I have continued to avail myself of every opportunity to visit the beautiful venue. As a consequence, my family and I have made many friends on the island over the years and are now well and truly accepted amongst the local community, a privilege we well and truly cherish. Both beach fishing and boat angling is a regular feature along the whole of the North Wales coastline which includes Rhyl, Prestatyn and Colwyn Bay. All of these areas I have enjoyed fishing from and each venue has always been most enjoyable and therapeutic, as well as having paid a

Author aboard a friend's for a day's fishing from Bull Bay

On our return to shore, 'Skippy' proudly shows off our catch of Tope

bonus of rich gastronomic dividends.

Eventually, I was able to move on from being a 'tiny' boat owner to owning a slightly larger vessel. This one also used a reliable Seagull' engine as its method of propulsion, and I deem it worthy of note to emphasise that not once have I had any cause to criticise the reliability and performance of any seagull engine' I have ever used.

As well as constantly reaping the savoury delights from my local shore and its adjacent tidal waters, I enjoyed visiting various locations where I caught a number of different varieties of fish. As I regularly spent annual holiday time with my family at and near to many seaside resorts, my son Ron also started to show a keen interest in fishing. From an early age I took him with me as often as I could and it was not long before he became quite a junior connoisseur with regard to catching, cleaning and even cooking the delightful specimens from the depths of the secretive Father Neptune's habitat. I sometimes travelled long distances from my Wirral home to other beach fishing havens such as Tenby and Saundersfoot down in South Wales, as well as enjoying deep sea fishing trips out into Cardigan Bay.

I had by now become a Police officer and also relished the regular boat outings as a member of my force's Police Sea Angling club. After a year or so I eventually replaced '*Swasie 1*' and bought my second boat which I named '*Swasie 2*' and although it was larger than its predecessor and had better (sheltered) facilities, it was not actually a boat designed for sea fishing too far out from shore, nevertheless, the vessel comfortably accommodated four for a day's angling. There was also room inside to shelter from driving rain if the weather became inclement, and should the need arise for us to make for our moorings at West Kirby in a hurry, the boat's big, reliable fifteen horsepower Johnson outboard engine was more than adequate to get us back safely. I was happy with my new boat and enjoyed a couple of trouble free years on many outings with friends and colleagues fishing the waters of the Dee estuary.

I was absolutely delighted with my new 'posh' boat which I must admit was not really a fishing boat at all. However, it was an opportune and affordable acquisition that I couldn't resist and one I considered ideal for getting me and a couple of friends out to do some serious boat angling. I

'Swasie 2'

had a friend who was an absolute 'mine' of information regarding anything whatsoever to do with the sea, especially the waters of the Dee Estuary and the Irish Sea, the late Harry Jones. Harry, like David Dodd (the writer of my foreword) was also a former RNLI Coxswain of the Hoylake Lifeboat which covered the whole of the Dee Estuary and Irish Sea as well as the Mersey estuary at the opposite side of the Wirral peninsular.

At the time Harry was also the boatman at West Kirby sailing club, a very up market and prestigious yachting establishment. What Harry didn't know about what was in any way nautical, wasn't worth knowing. He kindly offered to assist me obtain a mooring among the sailing club's boats 300 yards off shore. This afforded me and my friends an excellent facility to have the maximum time fishing the waters surrounding Hilbre Island, out in the Dee estuary. Harry's kindness also ensured that my boat, like those from the sailing club, would be safe under his and the club's constant supervision. If ever I had needed Harry's advice or assistance with any problem, he was always there to oblige. My West Kirby mooring was more than adequate to obtain maximum time out on the water. We could walk out and board the boat and then sit and await the incoming (flood) tide to float us off the 'chain'. After enjoying the full duration of the tide, we could then return to my moorings at the last of its ebb then walk ashore when the boat was 'dry'.

It goes without saying that, for safety sake, it is always essential to ensure an intimate knowledge of the sands and it gullies and channels. As previously explained, it would be most foolhardy to just wander out from the shore without such knowledge. It is of equal importance to be fully conversant with the times and heights of the tides' ebbs and floods. There have been far too many fatalities due to people not taking the trouble to know when the tide would come in and subsequently, many have been cut off by a fast incoming tide. Due to me being a 'local' and being blessed with friends with the knowledge and experience of the local shoreline and its behavioural patterns which they kindly were to pass on to me, I would always adopt a strict insistence with regard to adhering to the unwritten rules of safety whilst out on the shore or out in the boat.

The sandy shoreline of the Wirral peninsular has always been clean and reasonably safe close to shore. Sadly as time went on I found that the menace of Spartina grass started to put in an appearance here and there. This dreaded menace had, a long time before, absolutely killed off the amateur and professional fishing activities at the picturesque little Deeside resort of nearby Parkgate.

A Bustling And Scenic Parkgate Prior To The Arrival Of Spartina Grass

The 'ravenous', sand obliterating and beach consuming menace had, many rears earlier been introduced as an intended form of control but had quickly taken over and run riot, totally out of control with devastating consequences..

To show and emphasise the devastating power of Spartina, the following pictures show the resort as it was in days gone by when the sandy beach ensured uninterrupted enjoyment by children, fishermen and cocklers alike. The picture below shows the modern Parkgate as it is today where birds and wildlife are now the only ones who enjoy the area which was once a 'sandy beach'.

Early picture of shrimp boat landing its catch onto slipway at Parkgate

Original sandy beach at Parkgate prior to being taken over by Spartina grass

Cocklers loading at Parkgate slipway prior to Spartina 'invasion' (photo – Copyright Francis Frith Collection)

The same Parkgate 'beach' *as it is today*

Happily, eventually the venue is once again an extremely popular venue for visitors to enjoy.

Back to the shores of West Kirby and Hoylake, once the fearsome menace started to manifest itself, each year parties of local residents and beach enthusiasts would organise an enthusiastic yearly dig to try and eradicate this evil menace from the shore. Their efforts *were* rewarding and successful – at first!

Spartina grass, how the dreaded menace starts

Another well known name in the local (Hoylake) fishing fraternity is that of the Bird family. Some of them too have graced the decks as crew of the local RNLI Lifeboats. Many times I would go out fishing and shrimping with Ray and Gordon ('Gordy') Bird in their little wooden 'clinker' built boat when we would trawl the waters off Hoylake for much sought after shrimps, or fish, which they would then supply to the local fish shops in the area. The Bird's boat was small but well up to its task and extremely seaworthy, even in 'lumpy' water. It had little side decks and two 'Sampson' posts, one each side on its stern for attaching the small shrimp or fishing nets to for trawling and the boat was powered by a small but powerful outboard motor. Ray and Gordon had successfully used this vessel for fishing and shrimping for a number of years without any problems. Eventually, when the time came for them to sell the boat, I jumped at the chance to buy it *as well as its moorings on Hoylake beach* (I now had *two* sets of moorings).

My 'new' boat became ... 'Swasie 3'!

On taking over my latest nautical acquisition, I lovingly fussed over it and scraped, sanded, painted and varnished it as if I was its maritime 'Mother Hen'!

Chapter Seven

An Accepted 'Rose' among the 'Thorns'

By now I was a well and truly hardened cop and many times I took keen and enthusiastic colleagues for a 'serious' day's fishing out into Liverpool Bay. My forays out on the 'oggin' didn't just include colleagues and local friends. There were times such trips were even 'therapeutic' for those who came aboard purely to enjoy a day trip out into the bay.

One day whilst I was out on mobile Police patrol I was directed to a 'Domestic Incident' which involved a seriously injured young boy. On arrival at the house I found a dazed, very badly injured and highly distressed lad in his early teens staggering about his front garden. I went to him and took him back into the sanctuary of his home. The boy (*who I shall call 'Danny',* which is not his real name) had been in school during the morning and his class were having a science lesson. After the lesson concluded at lunchtime Danny came home for his mid day meal which had been left out for him by his parents who were at work for the day. After consuming his meal Danny then went outside to an outhouse and tried to re-enact and emulate what he had learned from the science teacher during the science lesson earlier that morning which was – how to make explosives! To prevent any young reader even *thinking* of trying to do what Danny attempted, I won't describe exactly what 'Danny' set about doing. However, to emphasise the gravity of what Danny did I will certainly describe the *consequences* of his folly. During his attempt to replicate what he had been taught earlier in the classroom at school, Danny proceeded to do this and do that, thinking he was performing the same skills as his teacher. Suddenly there was a violent explosion which blew Danny across the room ripping his arm off as well as inflicting other serious injuries and almost totally destroying the outhouse. Thankfully, 'Danny' remained conscious and was able to perform a miracle by staggering back into the house to dial 999. On hearing the loud bang, a neighbour immediately rang the police and as I was in the close vicinity, I was at the scene within a couple of minutes. I rendered what first aid I could and retrieved the boy's severed arm and to save time, as there was no sign of an ambulance, I placed him into my police car and sped off to the casualty department at Walton Hospital where the boy was admitted for immediate emergency surgery. Sadly, his shattered arm could not be replaced and the remains were cleanly amputated above his elbow.

I left the hospital to locate the boy's parents and returned with the highly distressed and shocked couple as soon as I found them at their place of work. After this, I made daily hospital visits to Danny with comics and books and sat chatting to him at his bedside as he slowly made progress over the forthcoming weeks. On his eventual release from hospital, (against 'normal protocol') I continued to visit young Danny at his home almost daily. I soon became a firm friend of Danny and his charming parents and I constantly monitored his progress during his very lengthy recovery. As my son Ron was the same age as Danny, I took him over to meet him and they were to soon form a close friendship which was also extremely 'therapeutic' with regard to enhancing young Danny's morale as he slowly came to terms with being an amputee. Eventually Danny was fitted with a prosthesis (false arm) which, sadly, was not to prove very successful.

One day, after a day's fishing, Ron and I went to Danny's house on the outskirts of Liverpool and delivered some of our catch so that he and his family could enjoy a meal of freshly caught fish. His parents were absolutely delighted and thanked me profusely. As Ron and I sat chatting with our hosts over the proverbial cup of tea, Danny inquisitively asked me about my boat and when and where I went fishing. His relentless questions and deep enthusiasm about boat fishing at sea and life on the shore resulted in him asking if he could join my son and me the next time we ventured out for another day's fishing. Needless to say, I was *more* than happy to oblige.

Danny's parents were delighted at his keen enthusiasm to get out and about and become engaged in some form of activity and were more than keen to encourage him. As a result of Danny's enthusiastic request, he became a regular member of my boat's fishing 'crew'. Danny's pedantic enthusiasm knew no bounds and in no time he was able to perform most of the tasks that

Ron and I did. This undoubtedly enhanced Danny's confidence and led to his speedy acceptance and recovery from his disastrous experiment. Eventually his regular, keen participation in fishing, shrimping and cockling with Ron and I out on the shore and at sea appeared to slowly bring Danny's life almost back to 'normal'. A close bond manifested itself between Danny and my son which exists to this very day, many years later.

Author's son Ron and 'Danny' at the boat on its Hoylake moorings

'Swasie 3', the former boat of the Hoylake fishing brothers Ray and 'Gordie' Bird gave me too, as it did with them, a number of year's reliable enjoyment as I continued fishing the Dee Estuary. As time went on my wife and I were blessed with a baby daughter Joanne, who, like her big brother Ron soon became acclimatised to the shore and the sea. As with Ron a decade and a half before, every time I went out to retrieve fish from my lay-lines, (day or night) I *had* to take young Jo along with me. At the start, like Ron when he was very young, Jo would be perched on my shoulders holding as torch while her 'Daddy' took the fish from the hooks and put them into a sack. As soon as Jo found her little 'sea' legs, she too accompanied Ron and I out on our shrimping and fishing trips in Swasie 3. Jo became adept to cockling and was a good little helper picking and bagging the cockles and on our return home she would be equally helpful helping me to cook, pickle and pot them. Jo became so well known down on the shore, she was christened 'Cockle Lily' by the lifeboat crew and was known thereafter by that name by all the fishermen.

Whenever I went out onto the shore, Jo always insisted on coming with me with her little rake and carrier bag if I was cockling or to help me riddle if we were after shrimps. The weather's behaviour mattered not one jot. She insisted on accompanying me rain, hail or shine. As a consequence of a little

Little Jo helps her dad and brother's pal 'Jonno' secure the boat after a day's fishing

girl continually helping her dad either on the shore or out in the boat, the press became aware of her activities and one day we were intercepted out on West Kirby shore as we raked and gathered cockles in the pouring rain. My little cherub and I were interviewed and photographed and the story of little 'Cockle Lily' subsequently appeared in the widely read evening newspaper, the Liverpool Echo. Jo had become a local celebrity even before she started school!! After the story and picture in the Echo, a similar story and picture appeared in the Wirral newspaper. Needless to say, I was immensely proud of my little fisherwoman!

I eventually kitted Jo out with a full set of oilskins, and new wellies which from then on she referred to as her *fishing set*. These were far better to repel spray and would ensure her clothes were always kept warm and dry underneath. She was absolutely delighted with her latest 'attire' and

Press picture heading the story of 'Cockle Lily' out cockling with her dad

Jo in her new oilskins after another day's 'toil' on the shore

excitedly informed me that she now looked like a '*real* fisherman' in her new gear! (Pictured below.)

Whenever the weather looked like becoming inclement, even when out with her mum wherever they would go be it visiting or shopping, Jo would insist on wearing her 'Fisherman's set'.

As I was now a boat owner and was mixing with the boat fishing and shrimping fraternity whose boats were all mainly moored a mile up river at Thurstaston, I acquired a mooring there too. All of the Dee shrimp boats and fishing boats were moored in a channel which would run dry at low tide. Once the tide started to flood it quickly filled the channel enabling the boats to make off fishing and shrimping. Many would leave their moorings on the ebb tide to return on the ensuing flood tide. The moorings were only three hundred yards from the cliffs on the shore. At the top of the cliffs sits the

Dee Sailing Club, opposite the moorings

Dee Sailing club, yet another prestigious sailing establishment which offers a boat owner every need. Once my boat was on my new moorings, I joined the Dee Sailing club and settled in with my new yachting and sailing friends. Not only did the club afford all the facilities necessary for an ardent boat owner, but the club was also was a great venue for regular social events. As well as enjoying the company of fellow members out on the water, many times social evenings or celebratory events were held at the club to enhance the club's activities. Club members wanted for nothing and every facility and assistance was available on request. The club had a 'Moorings Officer', Mr Don Mackinnon an absolute officer and a gentleman. If I thought I knew a lot about boats and boating, Don certainly taught me a lot more! He was always at hand to give any assistance whatsoever if and when required.

Many times after a day's fishing, angling, shrimping, or even just out cockling, it was great to make for the club and if the premises were 'closed' I could let myself in to shower and change before driving off the club car park to make my way back home. The club was an absolute blessing and I have now been a member for over twenty years, a privilege I still enjoy to this day. As the years passed I progressed in my police career to grace the ranks of the Criminal Investigation Department (CID). To many, such a move was deemed as a '*promotion*' and an 'elevation' of status. Nothing is further from the truth! This popularly held belief is in fact a fallacy, it is simply a case of an officer who wishes to aspire to a preferred department of the service to apply and if selected and successfully completes the appropriate course, he or she will then cease to be a uniformed constable and will then become a detective constable. I was delighted to be accepted into the CID as this is what direction I wished my career to take. The reason I elaborate as to my entry into the CID is because it was due to my becoming a detective that it eventually inadvertently enabled me to move on to my next absolutely first class 'up market' boat.

In my first years as a detective constable I investigated numerous cases and serious crimes of every nature. During such investigations I arrested many felons and brought about their deserved incarceration. Some cases I successfully solved and some cases I didn't. Many of my successes enabled me to restore stolen property to their grateful owners.

Once such case involved the theft of some extremely expensive boat engines from a Liverpool boat builder's premises. This particular firm made boats that were very 'up market' and were mainly for export to rich customers in far Eastern countries. The premises were forcibly entered one night and the engines were removed by a vehicle or vehicles. As well as my other crime solving tasks of arrests and appearances at both Magistrates and Crown courts, as well as the formidable necessity of completing admin and mountains of paperwork, I gave this serious case (due to the amount of money involved in the theft of such highly expensive property) my undivided attention. After weeks of 'diligent sleuthing' I managed to get a breakthrough. My enquires finally led me to an address (a scrap yard) owned by a seedy character in a crime ridden and run down area. After receiving information from a reliable 'snout' (informant) I obtained a search warrant and a team of colleagues and I raided the premises where we executed a meticulous search of the yard, its buildings and surrounding area. Eventually, after removing thousands of bits and pieces, old bangers and debris, three of the five engines were discovered secreted in various places. The three engines, which were worth many thousands of pounds were subsequently photographed and returned to their rightful owners, the boat builders Arrests were made and the matter was subsequently dealt with by the courts and brought to a successful conclusion, although only three of the seven engines were recovered it was still deemed a successful outcome due to the high value of the property recovered.

As I wandered around the firm's premises after the case I was highly impressed and in awe of the extremely expensive vessels which were ready for export to numerous rich buyers in various countries abroad.

In another part of the premises I saw a number of empty, open hulls. The hulls were finished but devoid of any fittings. Many were partially full with rain water and contained various bits of debris. I asked why the hulls appeared to be so shoddy and unattended. The firm's managing director informed me that the hulls were 'seconds' and went on to inform me that such were his firm's extremely high standards, nothing short of one hundred per cent perfection of every part of each vessel's manufacture would be accepted. I asked what was to be the fate of the hulls I was seeing lying abandoned. He informed me that each and every hull would be destroyed. I looked at each one closely and the most I could find 'wrong' was a striation or unsightly mark somewhere on the hull. I found one hull and after I examined it closely found nothing more than a slight blemish. I pointed this out to the MD and he informed me that, yes, even such a small hardly visible blemish would still not be acceptable and the hull would be destroyed.

I asked if it would be possible for such a hull to be purchased but I was informed that the firm would only allow a 'perfect' product to leave its premises. I explained that, as a boat owner, I was keen to see if there was any possibility he could make an exception and allow me to purchase the hull. The managing director said he would put my (unusual) request before his board of directors and let me know in due course. The outcome of my unusual and no doubt audacious request was that, after due consideration,

I would, as a one off, be allowed to purchase the 'blemished' sub standard hull for a nominal price on the understanding that the name and place of its manufacturer would never be disclosed. I was ecstatic at the outcome of my request. The hull was delivered to my home and deposited on my front lawn. Once in situ and stocks put into place, a friend, John McCoy, a most competent and fantastic joiner, then commenced to bring my drawings to fruition and built the upper structure of the boat to my design and eventually, after a lot of hard work and 'midnight oil' was consumed, my 'new' boat was born. She was named after my little daughter, '*Cocklelily*'. Now, as the boat building firm has ceased to exist for the past two decades I am no longer breaching confidence by proudly saying that my boat hull was made by none other than the number one boat builder, Stewart Stevens.

Once the boat was finished, another highly efficient and hard working local boat builder, Alan Tolley from Hoylake (another former RNLI lifeboat crew member) set about installing the boat's engine. This was an inboard 100E Ford engine which, from the outset was very reliable (even though it was a petrol engine). The new boat was an excellent sea boat and it also behaved perfectly in 'lumpy' water. It could comfortably accommodate four anglers and their gear and there was plenty of room 'below' for a proverbial cuppa and refreshments as well as it being a brilliant 'refuge' if the weather became inclement. Altogether I was not only very pleased with my extremely lucky purchase, but extremely grateful at the privilege of obtaining such a worthy vessel for such a low price. I am forever grateful to my joiner and boat building friends for their brilliant work converting an empty, unfurnished hull into a first class sea angling boat.

As my new vessel became a familiar sight amongst the local boats, the graceful lines of the 'new kid on the block', the new *Cocklelily* drew envious glances from some of my fishing and angling fiends. I was more than happy to oblige my fellow sailing club members by ferrying or transporting various items to and fro and I especially enjoyed transporting bulky items out to the West Hoyle bank during the Dee Sailing club's annual 'Commodore's Cruise'. This most enjoyable yearly outing is when the club ventures out into the Dee Estuary and sets up a bar and barbecue on the large dry West

Hard work complete. The finished product

Jo and her namesake, The new 'Cocklelily'

Hoyle sandbank. There, we enjoyed many hours sunbathing, drinking and consuming barbecued (freshly caught) fish, steak, sausages and all the rest of an equally gastronomic fare cooked on the hot charcoals. Hours later, as the tide turned and started to flood, we would return to our moorings and each of us would make to shore in our tenders and head for the club to conclude an extremely happy and most popular annual club's event. As a member of the club, my profession was accepted amongst the other sailing club's various professionals, indeed many other members were also police officers, firemen or members of the other emergency services.

However, I don't think that 'cops' are the most popular 'beings' amongst the tough, rough and tumble men of the fishing fraternity who at the most would probably reluctantly tolerate them, but I am proud to say that I have *always* been totally accepted and have enjoyed nothing less than an excellent relationship with all those fishermen, shrimpers and cocklers out there on the Wirral shoreline. Maybe it is one of the privileges and benefits of being, like them, born and bred almost on the shore with salt in my veins?

Chapter Eight

Broadening the Horizon

Boat angling certainly broadens the spectrum of fish to be caught as opposed to that of beach angling. The varieties of fish which can be caught from a boat are virtually endless. Although my fishing trips out into the Dee estuary usually furnished 'flatties', whiting or perhaps an eel or two, once out into the expanses of Liverpool Bay, the variation would further increase to other fish such as cod, codling mullet or sea bass. The sea bass provides an extremely delightful fish menu to enhance many enticing dishes, having a most exquisite flavour and its texture is very moist. They are great when lightly stuffed and grilled, then their delicious skin becomes crisp but the fish remains succulent and tender.

Again, an enticing bait for catching bass is Lug worm, Rag worm or strips of mackerel. Sea bass are caught from shore too, especially in the surf. This fish can furnish many dishes for the reader to enjoy, as I have on many occasions. Below is a mouth watering selection of menus which may be of interest to whet the appetite of those enthusiasts who enjoy sea food dishes.

Gastronomic delight, the very popular Sea Bass

Crispy Grilled Sea Bass

One 3 lb Bass
1 orange
2 sprigs of dill or parsley
1 tablespoon of lemon juice
Small (1 inch) piece of root ginger
2 tablespoons of soy sauce
4 tablespoons of sunflower oil
Salt and freshly ground black pepper
Garnish the dish with lemon wedges

Method

- Cut off the fins with scissors. Take a sharp, pointed knife and cut behind the head slide the knife down the length of the fish alongside the backbone. Repeat the same procedure on the other side to release the whole backbone. Using scissors, sever the backbone from behind the head and in front of the tail, remove the bones, then gut and clean the fish from the other side.
- Remove the peel and pith from the orange and cut the flesh into slices. Season the inside of the fish with salt and pepper and stuff it both sides with the orange, parsley and half the lemon juice. Score the skin of the fish with shallow diagonal cuts. Peel the ginger root, chop it roughly then squeeze it through a garlic press. Rub the cuts in the sides of the fish with the ginger juice, the soy sauce and the remainder of the lemon juice.
- Heat the grill to its hottest, line a tray with foil, brush it with oil, place the fish onto the foil and pour the remaining oil over it. Grill the fish as near as possible to the heat for 7 minutes, turn it over and grill the other side for a further 4 or 5 minutes. Test by poking the fish with a pointed knife to see if the flesh in its centre is opaque, do not overcook. Serve at once with wedges of lemon and pour over any juices from the pan.

A Dish of Grilled sea bass

Baking in salt is another good way to cook a whole sea bass. The salt crust acts as a seal so the fish becomes succulent and tasty but not salty.

Other ways of cooking a whole sea bass are roasting in the oven, or barbecuing. Both of these methods are best by tightly wrapping the fish in tinfoil first. To enhance the flavour add oil, butter herbs, vegetables or citrus fruit.

Also, try deep frying bass fillets in a light, airy butter, very tasty! Like most fish dishes, the enticing lists of menus and cooking methods are varied and endless.

Even though I was now a boat owner, I still maintained my activities on the shore raking and collecting cockles, picking mussels, gathering periwinkles and the tasty razor fish and also, my ever enthusiastic and keen pushing my net for the ever sought after shrimps. I would sometimes wear waders for this, but I also preferred wearing my oilskin leggings and trainers as I found I could push my net out into deeper water, even up to my neck sometimes, but my 'unusual' preference many times paid dividends by filling my net with shrimps. My outings to push for shrimps were not restricted to warm, sunny days, as I was equally enthusiastic to pursue the delightful crustaceans during cold and wet nights. Many times I found netting in the darkness to be more beneficial? There is nothing better than seeing the shrimps jumping out of the water ahead or your net. On seeing this, you know that you know you are in for a bonanza of a catch.

Shrimps are an extremely popular and delightful form of cuisine and they, like wet fish, can furnish a very wide and much enjoyed number of menus and dishes. When trawling for shrimps in a boat they are usually boiled aboard in sea water.

Boiling the freshly caught shrimps in sea water aboard

However, when pushing for them, I would return home with my day's catch and boil them in salt water. I ensured a regular salt supply from my nearby fish and chip shop and I had a large bottled gas fed copper boiler which was more than adequate to cook whatever amount I brought home.

The method of cooking shrimps is by placing them into boiling water, which will take it off the boil, then wait until the water comes back to the boil and remove shrimps after three or four minutes. If they are boiled for too long they become too soft and difficult to shell (pick).

Peeling (or 'Shulling' as we locals pronounce it) is relatively easy and practice makes perfect as the saying goes. To shell the shrimp take hold of the head with one hand, holding it between the thumb and index finger and similarly take hold of the tail with the same fingers of the other hand. Gently push the head and tail towards each other in a telescopic fashion then reverse

The author with a large catch during his nocturnal push for shrimps (Note water mark up to his shoulders on his jacket indicating depths he has pushed!)

A Live shrimp

Shrimp cooked ready to be shelled (peeled) for eating

by pulling the tail section away. This should come away easy to reveal the flesh of the shrimp. Discard the head and tail and there you have the shrimp ready to grace the plate. The shrimp is so easy to enhance any appetising dish; I will add a further couple of recipes to assist the ardent chef.

Shrimp Fried Rice

Ingredients

3 tablespoons of soy sauce
1 tablespoon of sesame oil
Half a teaspoon of ginger powder
Half a teaspoon of white pepper
2 tablespoons of olive oil
One pound of peeled shrimps
Salt and freshly ground black pepper to taste
2 cloves of crushed garlic
1 onion, diced
2 carrots, peeled and grated
Half a cup of frozen corn
Half a cup of frozen peas
3 cups of cooked rice
3 green onions, sliced

Method

- Whisk together the soy sauce, sesame oil, ginger powder and white pepper in a small bowl and set aside. Heat the olive oil in a wok or large skillet over a medium heat. Add the shrimps and cook for about 2 to 3 minutes, stirring occasionally and season with salt and pepper then set aside.
- Add the garlic and onion to the skillet and cook for 2-3 minutes, stirring often until the onions have become translucent. Add the carrots, corn and peas and stir constantly until the vegetables are tender, about 3 minutes. Add the rice, green onions and soy sauce mixture and cook for two to three minutes, stirring constantly until heated through then add and stir in the shrimps. Serve immediately.

Another, easy to cook and prepare appetiser is ***Easy Shrimp and Broccoli Stir Fry***.

For this you will need

1 tablespoon of olive oil
One and a half pounds of peeled shrimps
Five cups of Broccoli florets
One teaspoon of sesame seeds
A green onion, thinly sliced

and for the sauce

3 tablespoons of soy sauce
2 tablespoons of oyster sauce
1 tablespoon of red wine vinegar
2 tablespoons of brown sugar
1 tablespoon of freshly ground ginger
2 cloves of freshly crushed garlic
1 teaspoon of sesame oil
1 teaspoon of cornstarch

Method

- In a small bowl, whisk together the soy sauce, oyster sauce, red wine vinegar, brown sugar, ginger, garlic, sesame oil and cornstarch. Heat the oil in a large skillet over a medium heat. Add the shrimps and cook for two to three minutes, stirring occasionally. Add the broccoli and cook for another three minutes until tender, stirring frequently. Stir in the soy sauce mixture until well absorbed and combined and slightly thickened, this will take another minute or two.
- Serve immediately, garnished with sesame seeds and green onion.

Although these are but a couple of recipes, the amount of further gastronomic shrimp delights is endless.

I also must add what a magnificent meal prawns can bring about, although all the time I have netted for shrimps, be it out in the boat trawling or hand netting from the shore, I have only ever been fortunate enough to have caught the occasional prawn or a very few prawns in the net, but never enough to furnish a decent feed! I don't ever recall any of the local fishermen netting prawns as their catches were all shrimps or fish. However, as I have always liked prawn dishes, here is another 'gem' for the table from the creative kitchen.

A live Common Prawn

Common Prawn, cooked

Curried Prawn Bisque

Below, the picture of the easily created dish which can grace any table on any occasion. The prawn is not as easy to pick (shell) as the shrimp as its shell is not as tough and easy to pull apart. However, although a little bit more 'fiddly' to remove than the shrimp, the prawn shell can be removed quite easily with a little patience.

The aromatically enticing end result, Curried Prawn Bisque

As you can see by the picture above, the creation of a fantastic curried dish is well worth the effort. The picture almost gives off an aroma by just looking at it. This was one of my mothers' and my wife's favourites. The flavour and taste is out of this world. For such a delightful example of sea food cuisine you will need the following ingredients.

2 oz butter
4 tablespoons of finely chopped onion
4 tablespoons of finely chopped celery
1 clove of garlic, finely chopped
3 tablespoons of plain flour

1 tablespoon of curry powder
A quarter of a teaspoon of paprika
1 tablespoon of tomato puree
2 pints of chicken stock
Half a pound of cooked prawns3 fluid oz of single cream
Salt and pepper to taste
1 tablespoon of brandy

Method

- Melt the butter over medium heat in large pan. Stir in the onion, celery and garlic and cook for five minutes or until tender. Mix in the plain flour, curry powder, paprika and tomato puree. Gradually add and stir in the chicken stock and bring to the boil. Reduce the heat to low and simmer for five minutes. Add the cooked prawns and then mix in the single cream. Season with salt and pepper to taste then add the tablespoon of brandy before serving.
- This is truly a real appetizing delight which is so easy to create.

Moving on to another rare but wonderful 'Bonus' I have been amazed and delighted to recover from my nets. The Edible Crab.

On *very rare* occasions when I have out boat trawling or hand netting for shrimps, I have unbelievably had the added, rare bonus of retrieving an edible crab from my net. Like the shrimps and other shellfish, crab too provides an excellent creation or addition to any sea fish meal. Crab sandwiches provide a delightful snack that cannot be bettered.

To cook an edible crab is basically the same method and procedure as that of cooking the shrimp or prawn. Place the crab into a pan of *boiling* water, and cook for approximately three of four minutes on the boil. For the information of the reader, Edible crabs, like all crabs can easily be identified as either male of female (Cock or Hen). When the crab is turned over, it reveals a 'purse', which is in fact a turned in tail. The broad tail is that of a female, the narrow purse is that of a male.

The very tasty Edible Crab

As I am furnishing my pictures and scriptures with various recipes for the fish I continued to catch it would certainly be remiss of me not to include a couple of recipes for this delightful addition to the chef's list. Below are two such recipes that I am more than confident will satisfy the taste buds of all who enjoy sea food cuisine.

Crab And French Bean Salad

Ingredients

8 oz of young French beans
2 firm, ripe tomatoes
3 spring onions
2 hard boiled eggs
3 tablespoons of olive oil
1 tablespoon of white wine vinegar
Half a teaspoon of Dijon mustard
A few drops each of Worcestershire and Tabasco sauces
1 tablespoon of tomato ketchup
1 roughly shredded crisp lettuce

Half a cucumber cut into thin two inch sticks
8 oz of white crab meat
Salt and freshly ground black pepper
Garnish with six black olives

This will be better in the spring or early summer when French beans are small and tender.

- Top and tail the beans and cook them in boiling salt water for six minutes until tender. Drain and rinse at once in cold running water and pat dry on kitchen towelling. Cover the tomatoes with boiling water for half a minute, drain then slide off the skins and slice the flesh thickly. Trim the spring onions and cut into four, lengthways. Shell and quarter the hard boiled eggs.
- Combine the oil, vinegar, mustard, sauces and tomato ketchup in a screw topped jar, season with salt and pepper and shake well to mix. Arrange the lettuce in a shallow serving dish and place the cucumber, tomatoes, egg quarters and spring onions around the outside. Pile the beans in the centre and spread the crab over the beans. Pour over the dressing, garnish with the olives and serve chilled with crisp French bread.

Cream Of Crab Soup

A gorgeous soup to set off a dinner party.

Ingredients

Fish stock *Made of the following. One large onion, peeled and sliced, 2 sticks of roughly chopped celery, 2 carrots peeled and sliced. One and a half teaspoons of mixed herbs, 2 cloves, 12 peppercorns, 2 bay leaves, 6 sprigs of parsley, one and a half tablespoons of salt, 2 lbs of fish bones and heads and 3 pints of water. Combine ALL the above ingredients in a large pan, bring to a vigorous boil and then simmer, covered for an hour. Strain the liquid before using.*

3 oz of butter
1 onion, peeled and chopped finely, 2 carrots, peeled and chopped finely
2 stalks of celery, chopped finely, 2 tablespoons of tomato puree
2 pints of fish stock (above)

1 pound of crab meat, half white and half brown
1 teaspoon of Dijon mustard
9 fluid ounces of medium sherry
5 fluid ounces of double cream
2 teaspoons of brandy
Salt and freshly ground black pepper and a pinch of ground nutmeg

Method

- Melt the butter in a large saucepan. Add the onion, carrot and celery and cook over a low heat, stirring to prevent browning, until the vegetables are soft. Add the tomato puree and mix well. Gradually blend in the stock, bring to the boil and boil over a high heat for 15 minutes until the liquid is reduced by a quarter. Add the white crab meat, mustard and sherry, season with salt and pepper and a pinch of nutmeg and simmer for 10 minutes. Strain off and reserve the liquid and puree the vegetables and crab meat through a fine sieve or food processor. Return the puree to a clean pan with the cooking liquid, brown crab meat and cream and heat until very hot. Pour into serving bowls and pour a little brandy over each bowl before serving.

When dressing the crab, first, remove the claws and legs, then prize open the shell and remove the meat from the inside the upper half and place into a bowl. This is easily done by means of a teaspoon or fork. However, to gain access to remove the flaky white meat from inside the bony skeleton of the lower half is a different matter. First, it is extremely important to ensure that the feathers (the 'lungs' or gills) are safely removed from around the outer sides and discarded. When this has been done, before proceeding to scoop out the contents from inside the thin bony structure, split this open to gain access to the white meat inside. This is best done my placing a heavy, sharp knife blade onto the top in the centre and pressing down firmly to slice open and split the skeleton into two pieces. Then, begin the delicate time consuming task of picking the tasty white meaty contents from the inside. For this a narrow pointed pick or skewer would be a perfect tool. Take extra care when doing this as it is easy to inadvertently include bits of the fragile shell amongst the meat as you withdraw it from the centre of the inner structure.

The legs of the crab too contain plenty of tasty meat which is easily obtained by snapping the legs in two and removing the meat from inside. The claws and joints also contain large amounts of meat but to remove this, you will need to place the claws onto a board or tray. I always find that striking the hard claw shells sharply with a Rolling pin, heavy knife handle or other heavy blunt utensil will crack the shell sufficiently to enable opening to remove the meat from inside. When all this is done, a decent sized crab will provide a large amount of meat which I place into a bowl and gently mix the leg and claw contents with the rest of the meat into a texture ready to scoop onto a plate or sandwich. The end result after all the hard work is well worth the effort to furnish an appetising and deliciously tasteful meal.

Cooked Crab with top shell and gills removed and claws cracked

Other fish I have caught over the years include mullet, coalfish, cod, dogfish (a small shark), garfish, gurnard, ling, Pollack, pouting, tope (shark), whiting and other species. As we move on I will elaborate on my various catches from the beach and the boat as to how I dealt with those I kept. Many I threw back into the water to fight another day! I will also illustrate some which made splendid dishes and I will share more of the delicious recipes regarding them. As much as I enjoyed sea and boat fishing, I also maintained my enthusiastic harvesting of the various edible shellfish to grace the plates of numerous dishes.

Chapter Nine

Some Others keen on Sea Food Meals

On the shore and also when out in the boat, it is not just the fisherman who is out for a day's catch to enhance his supper. Many times competition is fierce when it comes to setting out to abate hunger! Competition comes in the way of hungry and determined sea birds of many species. Some are even aggressive when it comes to obtaining their supper.

A gull that is easy to identify is the black headed gull. This bird is extremely agile in flight and it can perform amazing manoeuvres to turn and dive down to snatch any item of food he spots with his amazing eyesight. They also hover, twist and turn as they follow boats while the crew is busy gutting and cleaning, throwing the tasty bits overboard. A smaller cousin if his is the 'Lesser' Black headed gull which is about the size of a herring gull but, amazingly its general predatory habits are similar to the big Great black backed gull which is easy to recognize. The Great black backed gull is very large and has a broad, black back and pink legs. It is a fierce and aggressive bird and other gulls keep well away from it. The bird will swoop and snatch small unguarded gull chicks and it will attack a variety of gulls in its quest for a meal. It has been known to take small rabbits and rats. Another regular resident of our shoreline is the Common gull which is similar in size to a herring gull.

Although the shoreline is the gull's natural habitat, nevertheless, they are sometimes deemed an absolute menace by some. They swoop and snatch ice cream and steal food from people who sit enjoying a picnic as well as even stealing from enthusiastic anglers who are careless enough to leave their catch unsupervised as they cast into the waters.

People are even prosecuted for feeding gulls by local councils who deem the birds an environmental nuisance due to their foraging in litter bins and leaving a pungent mess everywhere to the expense of those who will have to clean up after them.

A Gull feeding on Periwinkles from the rocks

The penalty for kindness

For those who insist on furnishing an ornithological treat to the ever hungry gulls, many are either placed before a court or handed an instant fine for disobeying the many signs informing that feeding the birds is forbidden. In such cases it may be that 'Kindness is a sign of weakness' as the saying goes?

Herring gulls gather whenever and wherever there is the slightest possibility of food. When the boats are out fishing, or during gutting and cleaning the catch of fish, or when, after riddling and returning the smaller shrimps back to the water, the gulls feed richly. An example of such a flying feeding frenzy is perfectly illustrated in the picture below of my local pal, the extremely well liked (and sadly missed) Hoylake fisherman friend of *everyone*, the late 'Stevie' Armitage. Steve is returning to his moorings after a successful day's shrimping out in the Dee estuary in his boat 'Dark Star'. Once back securely on the moorings he would then boil and riddle the remainder of the catch before bagging all ready to take ashore. Steve, like the rest of the local

The late 'Stevie' Armitage returns with Dark Star and its day's 'Bounty' of fish

fishermen, was a regular supplier of fresh fish to the shops and pubs in the area with his much sought after fresh fish and shrimps.

People often moan and criticize the price they have to pay for fresh fish but many times, the effort to get fresh sea food onto the fish shop slabs is certainly no easy task. Many times I have witnessed atrocious weather suddenly arrive without warning against what had been previously forecast. When such a scenario presents itself things can suddenly become dangerous to say the least. In my case, when such inclement weather was the case as, an alternative to going out in my boat I would go onto the shore to either gather cockles or enter the shallows to push my hand net for shrimps. However, for a professional fisherman such an alternative doesn't enter the equation. If the weather prevents a boat from going out to catch fish, the fisherman who depends on fishing for a living will almost certainly lose out considerably and financially.

Such an example of atrocious weather which can *many* times prevent the fisherman earning his 'bread and butter' is pictured below. Even to another well known extremely hardy and greatly experienced Hoylake fisherman, Bob Beech, a well respected former RNLI Lifeboat crewman, common sense will *always* prevail over foolhardy enthusiasm to catch fish. Bob's boat sits on its mooring straining at its chain off Hoylake as ferocious gales lash the North West coast. It goes without saying; this is obviously one of those 'No Go' days for all who depend on the sea for their living.

As well as Bob being a very able and experienced boat owner and highly skilled fisherman, he also became the 'Captain' of another of Hoylake's highly prestigious and extremely popular 'watering holes', the Plasterers Arms public house. This pub has been a favourite gathering place of the local fishing fraternity for generations and when Bobby Beech took over as licensee, this seemed to be a very appropriate and apt position for one of Hoylake's very own to occupy.

The premises were frequented by many and Bob was as an efficient pub landlord as he was a fishing boat skipper. Even during his time as pub licensee he still couldn't resist keeping his fishing activities and skills alive. Bob continued to make nets so that others could benefit from his skills. It

Hoylake fisherman Bobby Beech's former boat LESLIE rides out an atrocious storm

Happier times, the 'LESLIE's decks awash with fish

The Plasterers Arms, the local fishermen's' pub with a local fisherman licensee

doesn't take rocket science to see why Bob was an extremely popular pub landlord. However, the irresistible lure of the sea eventually enticed Bob back to his *real* way of life, his true forte', – fishing, so he bought another boat and resumed what came natural to him.

When I used to 'imbibe' I enjoyed many evenings with the lads there at the Plasterers. Sadly pub popularity has generally waned over the years due to spiralling costs etc but thankfully one or two of such local establishments still survive and remain for social gatherings in the area.

Another local and popular character who was also a Hoylake household name was Mick Ackroyd. Like Bob Beech, both would many times cause queues to form at Meols slipway to purchase a selection of fresh fish brought

Priceless and envied skills. Bob Beech making new nets during his period as the Plasterers' licensee

ashore by the duo. Bob's wife Noel too would assist at the very popular venue serving and wrapping the fish they sold to their enthusiastic customers, many of whom had come from far and wide for their freshly caught fish.

It is amazing how, over the years, the site of the Hoylake fishing fleet's moorings have had to move from place to place as the sand has filled and silted the channels.

It is not all that long ago that the large number of fishing boats graced the beach at Hoylake where a little jetty led out as far as the channel which would quickly flood on the incoming tide. Sadly, such a sight no longer exists as over the years the moorings area has silted up forcing a diminishing fleet to move further along until now only a (small) number of private pleasure boats and yachts together with just a couple of fishing boats are left at the far end of what was once a wide and deep channel. Like many who visited the popular resort of Hoylake, I used to dive into the water from the jetty which was a popular venue for visitors and locals alike. The sand bank is so high now that to get out to sea, even at full tide, boats have to negotiate a lengthy narrow channel for nearly two miles alongside the sea wall before turning to port and making out to sea. To add to this tale of woe, we now have the dreaded and highly invasive Spartina grass sprouting up all over the beaches which, in the not too distant future, will no doubt bring about another 'Parkgate'?

Hoylake was once a very thriving fishing 'village' which had a very large fishing fleet. Now there only a few full time fishermen who catch and sell their fish or shrimps or substitute their activities to cockle gathering. Cockling too has now become regulated to preserve stocks. The remaining stalwart fishermen are mainly moored at nearby Thurstaston but even there the channels are dwindling and Spartina is present.

The extremely popular venue of Thurstaston is two miles upriver from the sea but still allows boats from the beach's moorings easy access to the North Wales coastal waters and the open sea. Another Hoylake fishing family name of long standing, the Triggs, still fish and shrimp the river and its estuary. Their boat, the Provider was eventually replaced by the present 'Sea Fisher'. Although Mike and his son Chris regularly work together, young Chris too has a boat of his own, the EMMA which sits among the same moorings as his father's boat. The two, both still work out from the sheltered little sanctuary's moorings at Thurstaston.

The Provider was always busy fishing the Dee estuary when the shrimps were in abundance. Skipper and owner Mike now works equally hard with Sea Fisher to ensure an adequate supply of fish and shrimps is continually maintained to the many fish shops in the area. However, like the rest of the fishermen earning a living from the locality, Mike will resort to cockling (which is now strictly monitored to preserve stocks) as an alternative when shrimp numbers are low.

The busy, popular Hoylake beach and jetty in days gone by

The same venue today, the jetty and channel now long gone

Mike Triggs's former boat Provider hauling in its catch

On many occasions I too fished the area as the busy Mike and his co fishermen went about trawling for their catches.

Another extremely well known boat fishing the area was the Mark Anthony, owned by my friend of long standing Dave Dodd (the writer of the foreword to this book). The boat was a long standing 'resident' of the Thurstaston moorings and was also a regular and familiar sight either in the estuary shrimping or out at sea fishing.

Many times during the day or night I have ventured out for a day's angling or nocturnal shrimping in the comforting knowledge that I had the 'protective' Mark Anthony and its experienced skipper nearby should I have ever needed their assistance.

Dave, having once been a very able RNLI lifeboat coxswain for which his services duly earned him a well deserved MBE has since permanently hung

Mark Anthony on its 'choppy' moorings with skipper Dave Dodd in wheelhouse while out on deck, Dave's son Andy and 'Gordie' Bird riddle the day's catch

his nets out to dry. He now spends all of his time at the RNLI Lifeboat station offering his continual and valuable experience and services for the benefit of the up and coming volunteers.

I take this opportunity the thank Dave for his kind assistance afforded to me in the writing and compilation of numerous facts and incidents in this book. Dave and I have assisted each other over the years at various incidents and one particular sad incident was when the two of us 'joined forces' when I was a serving Police sergeant and Dave was the second coxswain of the Hoylake (deep sea) RNLI Lifeboat the Mary Gabriel. Although the boat itself was not needed on the occasion, Dave personally attended the scene without any hesitation to assist me.

I was on mobile patrol along the Wirral sea front at Moreton when I spotted a body floating in the sea. A few days before, two young anglers

Author awaits the arrival of Dave Dodd to assist the recovery of the body

set out in an open boat, inadequately dressed for open water fishing and tragically, neither returned from the trip.

On seeing the body I notified my control room of the tragic circumstances that prevailed and requested an ambulance. Within a very short few minutes, Hoylake Lifeboat (second) coxswain (at the time) Dave Dodd arrived and offered me his assistance. Together, we waded into the surf and recovered the body of a young man who was in fact one of the two missing anglers who had not returned from their angling trip a few days earlier.

Dave and I successfully dealt with the incident and the sad scenario was successfully and professionally concluded and the body was removed from the scene.

Off duty, my enthusiasm for the RNLI and Coastguard was such that I became a 'Volunteer Coastguard' and to add to this I also became a proud and fiercely loyal enthusiastic Royal National Lifeboats Institution 'Governor', both positions I continue to hold with pride and enthusiastic dedication.

Chapter Ten

When One Door Closes, Another Door Opens

I became an ardent and keen member of the Coastguard (Volunteer) and took my membership seriously. I befriended former local Coastguard Brian May who I would join forces with when I was on duty as a police officer if an incident occurred requiring our joint co-operation. I was privileged to mix my involvement both on (police) duty and when I was also off duty. I would *patrol* the sea front area of Wirral in my Landrover and check the boats etc during my leisure time so I had the privileged opportunity to utilize a continual supervision of all that went on and at the same time keep my eye on all the boats along the whole length of the coastline.

I took matters of safety very seriously regarding seamanship when I was out in the boat so I had attended the South Mersey College and successfully completed a VHF Radio course and qualified as a fully fledged radio operator. From then onwards I was able to maintain radio contact with the coastguard to keep them aware of my whereabouts, the number of people aboard my vessel and times of departure and return whenever I ventured out to sea. Now, I was also able to maintain radio contact with the authorities from my Landrover whenever I needed to inform them of an incident etc during my regular runs along the seafront as I checked the moorings and fishing boats out trawling through my binoculars. Once or twice these efforts bore fruit and I was able to have assistance rendered to those in need.

(The position, together with that of RNLI Governor, he still holds with enthusiasm).

I once again moved on from having 'Cocklelily' to acquiring another slightly bigger boat and took out police colleagues on regular fishing trips. Although a larger boat than the former Stewart Stevens glass hulled 'Cocklelily' the new boat's wheelhouse was little more than a cockpit! However, it was a very good seaworthy boat in 'lumpy' water. Its main virtue was it had a more powerful diesel inboard engine than that of a 100E petrol engine.

Former Coastguard officer Brian May

Author in his 'off duty' role as Auxiliary Coastguard Volunteer

The 'new' boat was given the once over by the extremely reliable and efficient Alan Tolley, a man who was not only a good friend but also a man in whom I had the utmost confidence so now I knew all was well with my latest vessel. As with my previous boats, each one not only gave me a lot of enjoyable fishing and angling trips, many times with friends and colleagues and this one was to be no exception. I not only enjoyed angling trips out with my friends, I concentrated more on trawling for shrimps when they were in abundance. I joined forces with the regulars out in the estuary. Although my net was nowhere near the size of those of the other boats, I nevertheless was happy with the small amount, in comparison to theirs, I brought ashore. The difference was that I would have to take my catch *home* to boil whereas the professionals boiled their catch aboard their boats. Nevertheless, I enjoyed my outings trawling for shrimps immensely. I named my 'new' boat 'COCKLELILY 2' after the apple of my eye, my lovely daughter Jo.

Author's daughter with the new COCKLELILY 2

Although still quite young, my daughter would regularly accompany me out in the boat shrimping or angling. She was no stranger to either as she, like me had become an ardent and keen beach comber, cockler and fisherwoman from when she was a toddler. Indeed, she had always been far more enthusiastic than her big brother Ron. I was now becoming inundated with requests from my police colleagues to take them out fishing whenever the opportunity presented itself. As a result, I now alternated between angling trips with a boatload of bobbies or trawling for shrimps with my daughter or other pals of the same ilk as myself. That particular day's fishing was very successful as we caught a number of fish that included a gurnard and two mullet amongst the usual assortment of flatties. Each and every one of those fish caught will furnish many wonderful meals and dishes.

Some suggested tasty recipes of those caught on the day are furnished below.

The new Cocklelily 2 with a couple of 'bobbies' aboard

Barbecued Mullet *(serves two)*

Ingredients

One large mullet gutted and cleaned with its head left on
8 tablespoons of sunflower oil
One and a half tablespoons of dried oregano
Juice of two lemons
Salt and freshly ground black pepper
Two tablespoons of freshly chopped parsley

Method

- Dry the fish with kitchen towelling and season with salt and freshly ground black pepper inside AND outside.
- Brush the fish with some of the oil, sprinkle with half the oregano and grill over a high heat, turning frequently, sprinkling the remaining oregano over the other side. Brush the sides as they cook with the lemon juice and remaining oil until the skin of the fish is crisp and slightly blackened and the fish is cooked through. Transfer onto a serving dish and sprinkle over the chopped parsley.

Mullet With Ginger *(serves four)*

Ingredients

1 whole Mullet cleaned and scaled.
2 spring onions, chopped.
One teaspoon of grated fresh root ginger.
Half a cup of garlic wine vinegar.
Half a cup of light soy sauce
3 teaspoons of caster sugar and a dash of chilli sauce.
Half a cup of fish stock
One green pepper, seeded and thinly sliced
One large tomato, skinned, seeded and cut into thin strips.
Salt and pepper
Sliced tomato to garnish

Method

- Rinse the fish inside and out and pat dry with kitchen paper. Make diagonal slits on each side of the fish then season with salt and pepper inside and out. Place the fish on a heatproof plate and scatter the spring onions and ginger over the top. Cover and steam for ten minutes or until the fish is cooked through.
- Place the vinegar, soy sauce, sugar, chilli sauce, fish stock, pepper and tomato into a saucepan and bring to the boil, stirring occasionally. Cook over a high heat until the sauce has slightly reduced and thickened. Remove the fish from the steamer and transfer to a warm serving dish. Pour the sauce over the fish, garnish with the tomato slices then serve immediately.

Baked Mullet

Ingredients

One Mullet fish
Butter
Parsley sprigs
One onion, sliced thinly
Salt and Pepper
White wine

Method

- Gut and skin the fish then remove its head.
- Butter a roasting pan that will just take the fish then spread three or four sprigs of parsley, some of the thinly sliced onion and sprinkle some salt and freshly ground pepper into the pan. Put the fish in and lay more sliced onion on top.
- Add a little more salt and pepper then pour about a quarter of a pint of white wine over all then dot with more butter and tightly cover with tinfoil.
- Bake in a moderate oven for about 20 minutes per pound.
- Serve with mashed, new or plain boiled potatoes with peas or broccoli.

The extremely popular Mullet fish which can furnish a number of versatile dishes

The other fish mentioned, the Gurnard will also provide a most appetizing and tasteful meal. The gurnard is a very bony fish and care must be taken when handling and preparing for the pot. The end result however is well worth the meticulous care that must be taken. Once all this has been done, now for *another* gastronomic gem!

Gurnard with Toast and Tomatoes

Ingredients

Four gurnard fillets
One tomato
One tablespoon of chopped garlic
Two thick slices of bread
One tablespoon of red wine vinegar
One tablespoon of fresh chopped mint
Olive oil
Salt and Pepper

Method

- Rinse the fillets under cold, running water then pat dry with kitchen paper. Place them into a metal oven dish and sprinkle with some olive oil and chopped garlic. Season with salt and pepper

The bony, but very tasteful Gurnard

Now filleted and a highly desirable ingredient for the following recipe

- Bake the fillets in a pre heated oven at 365F (180C) for half an hour. In the meantime bring a pan of water to the boil. Add the tomato to the boiling water for 15 seconds then remove and cool under cold running water. Remove the tomato skin, chop the tomato and remove the seeds (pips). Keep one tablespoon of diced tomato aside for garnish.
- Put tomato flesh into blender and add red wine vinegar and olive oil. Pulse to a smooth vinaigrette then season with a little salt to taste. Pour blended tomato mix into a bowl. Add chilli powder and extra olive oil to taste. Mix well. Pour through a sieve and catch vinaigrette in a bowl. Chill it in a fridge until later. Toast bread slices and remove fish fillets from the oven.
- Put the toast onto plates, drizzle lightly with the tomato vinaigrette. Top with the cooked fish and sprinkle with more vinaigrette. Finish off with the sliced tomato and freshly chopped mint. Serve immediately.

Here are another couple of gems.

Red Gurnard, Spinach, Cockles and Shrimps *(serves four)*

Ingredients

Ten ounces of fresh cockles
Four gurnard fillets
Two shallot, peeled and finely chopped
Two fluid ounces of white wine
One tablespoon of chopped parsley
Three and a half ounces of butter
Two ounces of peeled shrimps
Two handfuls of spinach, trimmed and washed

Method

- Clean the cockles and check the gurnard fillets for any small bones.
- Place the shallots into a pan with the white wine and bring to the boil. Add the cockles and parsley, lightly season and cover with a tight fitting lid. Cook over a high heat for three minutes, shaking the pan to ensure the cockles open.

- Stir in a knob of butter with the shrimps, discard any cockles that don't open.
- Melt one and here quarters of the butter in a non-stick frying pan. Season the fillets and fry them skin side down over a medium heat for three minutes. Lower the heat then turn the fillets over and cook for two minutes on the flesh side.
- Blanch the spinach in boiling water for three minutes then drain well. Toss in a generous knob of butter over a low heat and season.
- Pile the spinach onto warm plates, lay the gurnard fillets on top and spoon over the cockles, shrimps and cooking liquor to serve.

Pan Fried Gurnard Fillets with Olive Oil, Caper and Tomato and Basil Sauce *(serves two)*

Ingredients

Two Gurnard fillets
One tablespoon of olive oil, for frying

For the sauce

Six tablespoons of olive oil
Four sliced tomatoes
One tablespoon of capers
One teaspoon of anchovy paste
Six basil leaves, chopped.

Method

- Place the olive oil and sliced tomatoes into a pan, bring to the boil then remove from the heat for five minutes to soften the tomatoes.
- Put the pan back on to simmer and add the capers and anchovy paste and leave to simmer while the fish gets cooked.
- Cook the fish in a frying pan on a high heat. Cook the fish SKIN SIDE DOWN for two and a half minutes then flip the fish over and cook the flesh side for the same amount of time.
- Turn off the heat and allow the fish to 'rest' for about a minute. Finish off the sauce by adding the chopped basil.

- Serve the fish on warm plates and spoon over the sauce and serve with boiled new potatoes.

The advantages of the COCKLELILY 2 were that it had a more powerful diesel engine which also enabled the vessel to engage reverse gear whereas the 100E petrol (car) engine did not and although I never experienced any trouble with the former, petrol engines are not a recommended form of power for a hard working sea boat. Nevertheless the former glass *Stewart Stephens* boat was an excellent and most seaworthy vessel which gave me *many* enjoyable nautical outings during my lengthy ownership. The problem with COCKLELILY 2 was the lack of wheelhouse space. The boat itself was of clinker built timber and

Limited space of Cocklelily 2 wheelhouse

extremely seaworthy, being heavy and lower in the water which made it more stable and had fewer tendencies to roll in swells or when riding anchor at sea.

I kept her for a couple of years during which she furnished many successful angling outings as well as enabling me to land numbers substantial catches or fish and shrimps.

Chapter Eleven

BOATS ... Bigger and Better – Moving up in the World

Eventually, after much thought regarding the lack of space I decided to seek a larger boat. I invested in a bigger and better boat with full accommodation. The boat was an 'Offshore Mirror', an extremely popular diesel yacht. Although I am not, nor ever have been, a *sail* sailor, this boat offered me everything I wanted and needed to pursue my enthusiastic fishing. Below, the vessel had two bunks, a flush toilet and small galley. Out on deck aft there was plenty of room for four anglers to enjoy a day's fishing. As far as I was concerned the boat fitted all my leisure and hobby's criteria. It was sheer luxury. Not only could I now go out for regular angling outings, I could now venture out for overnight trips to distant venues if I wished. The world was now my oyster! As I was a police sergeant in charge of a section, the rank which the Metropolitan police refer to as a 'Skipper', I set about painting the name of my new vessel the 'BLOCK SKIPPER' as I was the *Skipper* of my block (section).

Once I had finished adorning the boat with its name I set about having the radio installed together with a weatherproof dodger around the whole of the stern. As well as the standard fitted navigational lights I also added powerful lights to illuminate the aft deck (cockpit) area for night 'operations'. I was now totally under the anaesthetic nautical enchantment! I had two close pals who were always aboard my vessels as they were as keen sea fishermen as I was. Consequently, one or the other, or both, were now my regular 'crew' members whenever I decided to go out onto the 'oggin'. My moorings remained there opposite my sailing club (the Dee Sailing Club) but I was also blessed with being able to take the boat and place it in the club boatyard whenever I needed to do maintenance work or for it to sit out the winter storms. 'Skipper' had an extremely reliable and powerful inboard

The new Block Skipper on her moorings

Skipper's tender

Home comforts. Warm confines of Skipper's galley

diesel engine which was discreetly sited but easily accessible for maintenance work to be carried out. The added (natural) facility, (should the engine fail) was of course its sails *should I ever need them* to get me along.

After only a couple of trips out fishing in the new 'Skipper' with a couple of pals I decided one day to venture further out to sea and make our way out to fish at the distant Mersey *Bar* (near to the then Bar Lightship). Part of the 'ship's equipment' now included a thickly insulated ice box (together with its *deeply frozen* ice bricks each outing) to house and preserve our potential catch. After an hour or so riding at anchor, during which time we caught a few fish, suddenly Vinnie, one of our trio, felt a violent tug on his line. Eventually, after an exhaustive struggle he managed to pump his powerful aquatic opponent to the surface. All was then revealed, he had hooked a large, aggressive Tope (shark) who must have weighed about twenty or more pounds. Vinnie's violent aquatic adversary obviously just did not enter into the spirit of *our* day's enthusiastic angling activity!

The Tope is a much larger cousin of the Dog Fish or 'Bull Huss', as *both* are members of the shark family. They are fully cartilaginous and all have a skin that is like extremely abrasive sandpaper. Indeed, the skin is actually quite capable of rubbing wood smooth and can certainly remove *all* layers of skin with ease, as can the smaller dog fish, which when skinned, filleted and eaten is often referred to as 'Rock Salmon'. Dog fish (and sometimes tope) are deemed very tasty among some sea fish connoisseurs. I have many times caught and eaten dog fish and on the day we caught the large tope, my pal Vinnie was able to gaff his adversary and together, the three of us brought it aboard and dispatched it before it could inflict injury with its razor sharp teeth. My pal informed us he intended to create 'shark' steaks from his catch. After he skilfully skinned the tope (he'd certainly done that before) he cut enough such steaks to adequately share amongst the three of us. As I had many times before consumed and enjoyed 'rock salmon', I looked forward to trying the large steaks that were now available to us trio of anglers. Fishing out at the Mersey Bar was nearly always productive due to the many species which frequented the deep waters out there.

After Vinnie's exhaustive battle and his subsequent furnishing of the steaks, the three of us sat peacefully bobbing about on the swell enjoying the serenity of the isolation out there on the horizon. The only interruption via the deck loud speaker was the occasional radio traffic to or from the coastguard or other vessels on the channel 16 wavelength.

I decided it was about time we had a bite to eat so I went below to furnish us each with a most welcome bacon *buttie* and an accompanying mug of hot tea to celebrate our day's exciting catch. As we sat enjoying our butties and cuppa, Tommy Oram, the other member of our day's angling trio watched his rod kick and he subsequently caught and brought aboard a dinner plate sized plaice. My day's endeavours netted me a couple of flatties and a medium sized whiting ... to add to the tea and butties!

As it happened, once I had later tasted the tope steaks I wasn't really fussy on them as I thought they were rather bland. They certainly didn't compare with my preference for its cousin the dogfish (Bull Huss) or *Rock Salmon* as it is often referred as, whose flavour is quite the opposite and *very* tasty.

The aggressive Tope being brought aboard the new Block Skipper

Dogfish (Bull Huss) or Rock Salmon

The following is a tasty recipe that will create a delightful meal for two.

Marinated Dogfish with Green Salad

Ingredients

Dogfish fillets cut into 2 inch chunks
Olive Oil
White wine vinegar
One lemon
One clove of garlic
Fresh parsley and fennel
Salt and pepper
Marinade
Two tablespoons of olive oil
Two tablespoons of white wine
Juice from half a lemon
Crushed garlic
Chopped fennel
Salt and pepper

Method

- Place all above into a jar and seal tightly before shaking vigorously to thoroughly mix the marinade.
- Place the dogfish chunks into a bowl. Pour the marinade over the fish and mix until all is evenly coated. Cover the bowl with Clingfilm and place into fridge for two hours.
- To cook, heat a dash of olive oil in a pan then tip in the chunks of marinated dogfish and cook until golden brown, turning over once or twice to ensure they are evenly cooked (about five minutes). Serve on a bed of green salad leaves with a squeeze of lemon and a dollop of mayonnaise.
- Serve with crusty bread and butter

Dogfish fillets

Marinated dogfish fillets cut into chunks and ready to cook

Yet another tasty Dogfish meal is MARINATED DOGFISH WITH CHICKPEAS AND CARROTS which is similar to prepare but with the different accompanying ingredients. Like other popular sea food menus, the dogfish too can certainly furnish *many* variations of an excellent sea fish meal.

I was absolutely delighted with my new 'posh' boat and my pals also couldn't get enough sea time out and about fishing the deep waters outside the Dee estuary. My trips now started to include overnight trips down the North Wales coast as far as Anglesey and beyond. Two old pals became my regular crew. They were now either Tommy Oram, an ex fire-fighter with whom I had attended many incidents over the years during my police career in Liverpool. Tom lived near me and we went back a long time. We had attended traffic accidents, fires and many other serious, sometimes fatal incidents during our mutual time in the emergency services. Tom was a very able and competent person to have aboard as no job was beyond him, especially with regard to diesel engines. My other 'crewman' was another close pal who I had grown up with since childhood, Rob Slee, who also lived close to me. Every time I went out in my new 'Skipper' either, or both, would always be aboard. Rob was a ship's navigator of lengthy service so he was more than handy to have around during long night trips! Like Tom, Rob too was no stranger to getting his hands dirty if need be. Whichever of the two were out with me would ensure that I had nothing to worry about with regard to the running of the boat. Rob was also an experienced yachtsman so if and when the sails would be needed, he was the very man to be on hand. I wanted for nothing and was more that keen to get out fishing or visiting venues for overnight stays aboard my new little floating hotel or fishing boat, whichever role we would intend her to be.

Our first (maiden) trip out of the Dee Estuary took Tom and me down to the beautiful of Anglesey, an angler's and sea fisherman's true paradise. We made our first overnight's stay at Red Wharf Bay (Traeth Goch) where we enjoyed the warm hospitality afforded us both by the staff and local patrons of the Ship Inn which is adjacent to the nearby beach where we were moored for the night. The voyage down was most enjoyable and uneventful.

Ship Inn, Red Wharf Bay

Our overnight stay was most comfortable tucked up in our bunks down inside the warm confines of Skipper's cabin. After being rocked to sleep by the sound of the waves plip-plopping against the hull, I enjoyed a good night's deep slumbers. The following morning after rising to a beautiful dawn, Tom and I enjoyed a full English breakfast of bacon, egg and beans before deciding where we would move on to and visit next.

We decided to make out to sea for an early morning's fishing off Bull Bay. We obviously made the right decision as we caught a number of coalfish and a large Pollack. The coalfish is actually a cousin of the cod and the young coalfish are called 'billet'. The coalfish is easily recognized as they are black on the back and have bluey green sides with a silver belly. Its lower jaw has a little barbule (feeler) under its chin which juts out further then the upper jaw. Once again, our success was due to the tempting lure of our rag worm

A dawn awakening aboard Block Skipper

bait as we drifted about 'jigging' our lines up and down every few minutes to attract our quarry.

Fishing for coalfish is often best around dawn (or dusk) as they tend to rise to feed near the surface at those times.

Pollack are similar to the coalfish in that they too are dark with silver sides and a silver belly. They also have a protruding lower jaw. The average Pollack weighs about 5 lbs.

The Coalfish or '*Coley*' as it is mainly referred to, is a very popular fish enjoyed by many and is a main contributor to a vast number of dishes on the menu. However, my favourite dish of 'coley' is without doubt the old standby, the proverbial fish 'n chips. A variation of the standard theme, although a bit more effort is involved, is well worth it.

Coalfish

So here is one of my favourite forms of ***Coley 'n Chips***.

Ingredients

One fillet of Coalfish

Two tablespoons of fresh breadcrumbs

One egg

Half a tomato

Lemon wedge

Sprig of fresh basil

Salt and pepper, Sun flour oil for frying

Method

- Make large potato chips and place into a pan of COLD water. Place pan on high heat until the water boils. Reduce heat to a simmer for five minutes then drain the chips off and replace them into cold water for five more minutes then drain off once again before placing the chips into a plastic dish and putting them into a fridge for thirty minutes.
- After this pat chips dry then deep fry for five minutes. Pat dry on kitchen paper to cool and replace into fridge for a further thirty minutes (the chips will be given a final fry while the fish is being cooked).
- Spread the breadcrumbs onto a large plate and break egg into a bowl, season with salt and pepper then beat the egg to combine.

- Add enough oil to a non-stick pan to cover its base then bring to a medium heat. Draw the fish through the egg mix then pat the fillet on both sides in the breadcrumbs.
- Place the fillet into the pan and fry for three minutes on each side, at the same time put the chips into pan again to deep fry
- When breadcrumbs are golden brown and the fish is cooked transfer on to serving plate.
- Drain the chips on kitchen paper and add them to the plate. Garnish with sliced tomato, lemon wedge and sprig of fresh basil. You are now in for a gastronomic treat!

Another one of many coalfish recipes which is one of my favourites to satisfy the eager taste buds is

Grilled Coalfish Fillet with Blueberry and Red Wine Sauce

Ingredients

You will need a fresh fillet of coalfish with the *SKIN LEFT ON*
New potatoes
Two ounces of trimmed green beans
One tablespoon of fresh blueberries
Two tablespoons of red wine
Quarter of a teaspoon of sugar
Two ounces of butter
Salt and black pepper

Method

- Place the potatoes into a pan of cold, slightly salted water, bring to the boil on a high heat then reduce heat to simmer for 25 minutes until the potatoes are softened. After the potatoes have been simmering for twenty minutes put the blueberries, red wine and sugar into a small pan and heat on medium heat stirring occasionally until blueberries burst and form a lush sauce. Butter a non-stick pan and lay on the coley fillet, SKIN SIDE DOWN. Season fish with salt and pepper, lay butter on top side and cook under a moderate grill for five minutes

A dish of Coalfish and Blueberry sauce

until the fish begins to flake and is cooked. Fry the green beans for two or three minutes in butter with salt and pepper to season. Drain the potatoes and return them to empty pan with slight amount of butter then swirl the potatoes in the butter until they are all evenly coated.

- Place the fillet, potatoes and beans onto a plate then spoon blueberry sauce over fillet and serve.

Now for the equally appetising Pollack. How about this for a tempting recipe to try?

Parmesan Baked Pollack fillets

Ingredients

Four Pollack fillets
One red onion sliced into rings (some to rest the fish on)
One lemon, halved and cut into slices
Salt and black pepper
A pinch of paprika
One cup of Parmesan cheese
Olive oil (to coat foil)

- Place onto a baking tray and coat with oil to prevent it sticking.
- Place onion rings onto the foil then add the Pollack fillets on top of the onion rings. Add the salt, pepper and paprika and put the lemon halved slices onto the fish. Sprinkle the fillets with parmesan cheese (over the lemon) then place into oven and bake on 375F for thirty minutes.

The popular and tasty POLLACK

This is a really simple dish to create but the end result is extremely rewarding.

And now for another mouth watering and easy to prepare Pollack meal.

Fried Pollack Fillet with Spicy Potato Wedges

Ingredients

Eight ounce fillet of Pollack
Two tablespoons of vegetable oil
Two teaspoons of hot chilli powder
Salt and black pepper
Two tablespoons of plain flour
One tablespoon of olive oil
A large knob of butter
Two tablespoons of frozen peas
Lemon wedge and freshly chapped parsley to garnish
One medium to large potato, cut into thick wedges

Method

- Pour oil into a bowl and stir in the chilli powder and a pinch of salt to taste.
- Add the potato wedges and stir them around to evenly coat them with the oil mixture. Lay the wedges on a baking tray and pour over any remaining oil from the bowl.
- Cook for thirty minutes, turning halfway through the cooking.
- Scatter the flour on a plate and season with salt and pepper. Pat the fillet on both sides in the flour then shake off the excess flour.
- Pour the olive oil into a non-stick frying pan and add an ounce of butter then put on a moderate heat unti the butter melts. Cook the Pollack for about three minutes on each side.
- Bring the peas to the boil then simmer. Drain the potato wedges onto kitchen paper then put them onto a plate and assemble with the fillet and peas and garnish with the parsley and lemon wedge. Enjoy.

And now, another Pollack meal. Serves two.

Sauteed Pollack in Lemon and Garlic Butter

Ingredients

Two tablespoons of butter
Two teaspoons of crushed garlic
One teaspoon of lemon pepper
Two Pollack fillets
Lemon wedges

Method

- Melt the butter in a large skillet over a medium heat and stir in the garlic.
- Season the fillets on both sides with lemon pepper the place them into the pan and cook for ten minutes, turning them over halfway through cooking to brown on both sides. The fish is cooked when it flakes when tested with a fork. Serve with boiled potatoes, potato wedges of chips. Sprinkle with lemon juice before serving.

After a second night afloat Tom and I left our Anglesey 'fishing grounds' to make the long but most enjoyable trip back to our moorings at West Kirby on the river Dee. We timed our journey so that we entered the river on the last of the flood tide. This was so that we could do a spot of fishing on the chain to supplement our already healthy 'frozen' fish stock. As we sat bobbing about waiting for the tide to run off so we could walk ashore, I dished up another snack of bacon butties and the proverbial mug of tea. The only thing I caught while we waited to run dry was an eel at the last of the tide, which was duly skinned and added to the already healthy contents of our 'freezer'.

Tom and I continued to enjoy many trips along the North Wales coastline and the numerous scenic little bays of Anglesey were always regular ports of call. The places we visited for our overnight stays included our favourite fishing venues of Bull Bay, Cemaes Bay and Amlwch. Each of these venues

Tommy Oram, popularly known to all as 'The Bosun', relaxes on our return

Author giving boat a final cleanup before going ashore
(Note Dee Sailing Club in the distance)

offered splendid facilities 'ashore' where we would visit the local 'hostelries' for an enjoyable pint or two of 'grog'. We would usually end the evening with a fish and chips supper before returning to Skipper to bed down for the night. I found that Block Skipper catered for all our needs and we wanted for nothing. Not only did we enjoy numerous deep sea fishing trips but we also enjoyed the cuisine our catches provided. Many times our tasty 'dinners' out at sea or on various moorings, or even riding at anchor would consist of 'fish n fish, with fish!!

Among those keen anglers who accompanied us out on our sea fishing trips was my very own beloved late wife Marje. She enjoyed the occasional outings aboard when she even participated in some sea fishing herself. Whenever she caught anything Tom was always there to assist by unhooking her fish to place into the 'Skerries' box. I would then always know what I would be having for dinner that day when I got back home during those nostalgic days.

So versatile is the large range of dishes which can be furnished from the mackerel, and even though I have given mackerel recipes previously in the book, now we are with this fish once more, I can't resist giving another tasty recipe for this highly nutritious fish which is protein and vitamin rich and low in fat. This is a meal for four which I am sure will delight the sea food enthusiast.

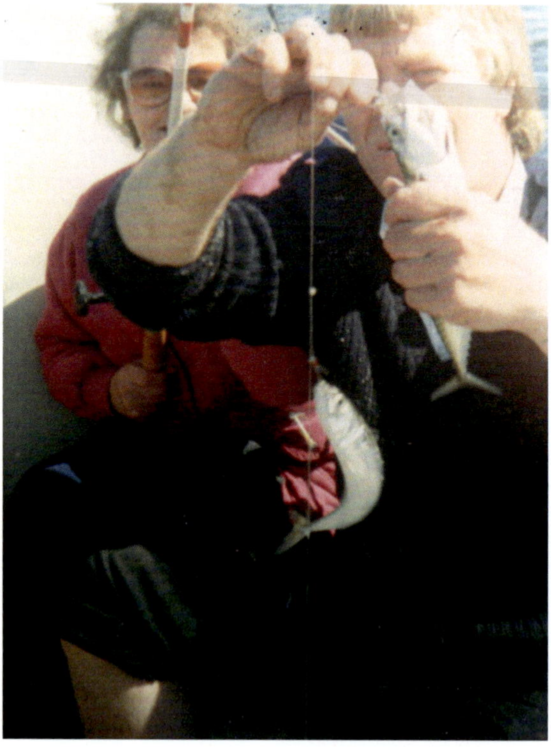

Tom retrieves Marje's mackerel catch

'Skerries' box containing bountiful catch of mackerel

Apple Stuffed Mackerel

Ingredients

Four large mackerel
Two eating apples
One onion
4 ounces (100g) Cheddar Cheese
Three ounces (75g) margarine
Two ounces (50g) fresh breadcrumbs
Half a teaspoon of cayenne pepper
Salt and pepper to taste
Oil to cook

Method

- Clean the fish and chop the cheese finely then peel and chop the onion finely.
- Mix half the cheese, apple, onion, breadcrumbs and cayenne pepper together, season lightly then bind with half the margarine.

- Stuff the fish with the mixture and secure the edges with toothpicks, dot with the remaining margarine and lay in frying pan with a little oil. Cook gently for ten minutes, turning once. Sprinkle the rest of the cheese on top and grill to melt and all is ready.
- BON APPETIT!

Although I have in the past, on very rare occasions, indulged in coarse fishing, my leanings have always been towards sea fishing from either the beach or a boat. Maybe this is because I have always been keen on sea *food?* I do however enjoy fresh trout or salmon, and have even tasted pike. There is a well known local exclusive coarse fishing venue not far from my home which is the *strictly* private waters of the Birkenhead Angling Club. The large pond is situate alongside the railway station at Meols near Hoylake. The club's rules regarding angling at the extremely well stocked pond are quite rightly *rigidly* enforced. Permitted attendance at this venue is strictly for club members only, even membership is restricted. Any unauthorised person found fishing

The scenic Meols pond

the site as a trespasser will be strictly penalised and prosecuted without any hesitation should he or she be found fishing at the closely monitored scene. Meols 'Pit' as it has always been known is a haven for the coarse fisherman. I would even deem it almost a local 'heritage' due to the abundance of varied wildlife that inhabits the beautiful scene. The whole area is also a treasured venue not only for the keen ornithologist but is pedantically protected by conservationists alike; the area is truly a local jewel in the crown.

Meols 'Pit' dates back to Victorian times and it is said that as the land was owned by the railways, the pit was dug and filled with water to enable the steam locomotives to take on water. Eventually the surrounding area of the pit became embroiled with thick, thorny vegetation and grass. As a consequence, the large area of water was rented out for a nominal fee to anglers who promptly set about clearing the sides of the thick undergrowth.

The anglers established their own club and the Birkenhead Angling Club were formed. One of the club's subsequent stalwarts is now the chairman of the B.A.C., Mr Harry Naylor. Harry and his team of keen, enthusiastic fellow members go out of their way to ensure a high standard is maintained in and around the whole area of what can now be considered a lake. The waters teem with fish of various species. Not least of these is the fearsome predator and worthy opponent of the keen coarse angler, the notorious Pike.

The fearsome Pike

There are a number of these who reside in the murky depths one of whom is reputed to be a 'giant' specimen?

Just for the record, for those who are fresh water culinary enthusiasts who may wish to try the following, I will include one such recipe for pike which I am sure will result in a very enjoyable meal.

Glazed Pike

Ingredients

One whole pike
Two tablespoons of cooking oil
Two bay leaves
Eight whole pepper-corns
One lemon, sliced
One cup of white wine
One ounce of Aspic jelly
Two cucumbers, halved and thinly sliced
Salt and freshly ground black pepper
Dill and Parsley sprigs with the lemon wedges to garnish
Mayonnaise, to serve

Method

- Wash the pike under cold running water and cut off the fins.
- Season the inside of the fish with salt and pepper then brush the skin with the oil to protect it from the heat while cooking.
- Place the fish on a rack in a large roasting tin. Add the bay leaves, pepper-corns and the lemon slices, pour over the wine and enough water to cover. Cover with a sheet of oiled tinfoil and bring to the boil then gently simmer for ten minutes.
- Turn off the heat and leave the pike to cool, still covered.
- When the fish is cool, peel off the skin. Prepare the aspic with boiling water then allow this to cool before brushing over the fish.
- Arrange the cucumber slices over the fish the brush again with the cool aspic.

A dish of Glazed pike

- Allow all to set then serve, garnished with dill sprigs, parsley sprigs and lemon wedges.

After my culinary digression, we now return to the cosmetic beauties of the Meols pit.

Other inhabitants of the pit include perch, roach and bream. The whole area is a scene of natural beauty and this is due entirely to the ongoing attention and pedantic maintenance of Mr Naylor and his team of keen fellow members of the Birkenhead Angling Club. Individual 'pegs' have been created into the banks and each year coarse angling competitions are held with keen participants travelling form far and wide to take part.

Membership of the club is kept to around thirty to protect the banks and their surrounding areas from being trampled by too many people. Mr Naylor and his team maintain a constant maintenance vigil to keep the lake clear of pondweed and also to ensure the protection of the wonderful wildlife that is constantly present. The 'fishery' will sometimes give an additional treat to the keen ornithological observer by the occasional visit of a beautiful Kingfisher seeking the opportunity of a meal. Other times the scene has been visited by exotic butterflies to further enhance the scene.

The beautiful kingfisher

The members of the Birkenhead Angling Club do a fantastic job in maintaining such an enviable Wirral beauty spot to such an extremely high standard. Is it any wonder they are so strict and determined to ensure that such a beautiful venue stays that way?

Now! Once again we move on from fresh waters back to the sea. My deep sea fishing outings and overnight trips with my ever reliable pal and crewman Tom continued unabated whenever the opportunity and fine weather presented itself. Tom and I took one or two close pals from our local pub, the Willows, after them frequently asking as they were keen to imbibe in the different and more rewarding hobby of fishing instead of propping up the bar! Those we took out really appreciated their nautical outings with the many times additional reward of them taking home a fish (instead of a liquid) supper!

None membership retribution

When Rob Slee came out in 'Skipper' he was always keen to become the efficient yachtsman that he is and hoist the sails to allow 'mother nature' to take over from our inboard diesel engine. In doing so Rob would 'come into his own' and we would be off for a day's journey to here or there under sail. Although I am not a yachtsman there is no doubt that travelling under sail is a very pleasurable experience. Relying on the elements and listening to the wind in the sails is certainly a most enjoyable way to spend the day.

It is surprising just how much distance can be covered and sometimes even faster than when under power. Even during the night as we were carried along under the stars to our various destinations, how could we fail to reach our intended destination with a qualified ship's navigator at the helm? I was so enthralled at such a most enjoyable scenario I painted such a scene of gentle tranquillity oils and framed the picture to hang on the wall of my home.

Author painted this scene of framed tranquillity in oils

As well as our enjoyable outings under sail, I continued with my enthusiastic fishing trips with friends and former police colleagues. Many of my pals were those who like me shared an insatiable hobby of life on the shore or out at sea bobbing about seeking whatever was to come aboard. The sheer pleasure of just wandering off around the beautiful Hilbre islands was enough for some who just wanted a day out on the water maybe just to photograph a seascape scene or the seals basking on the North Hoyle sandbank. For me, I would be trailing a line over the side or brandishing my fishing rod as the keen photographers took their pictures. The Dee estuary is a myriad of potential scenes for a budding photographer, especially for one who has such a golden opportunity of being is out and about there in a boat. I also would take pictures of fellow boat owners' vessels as they trawled for fished for shrimps or meandered out and about for a day's sailing and would converse with them over the radio. I found such a way life to be very relaxing and therapeutic after the stresses and strains of being a front line copper for over a quarter of a century.

Skipper' in tranquil waters off Hilbre Island (Author with passenger aboard photographing the beautiful Island and its birds)

At the end of each season, my boat would be taken out of the water and placed in the safe confines of my club's boatyard where I could clean and maintain it a leisure with the able assistance of Tom and fellow boat owner and club member Rob Slee. Being 'laid up' on the club's secure premises during the winter months not only offered safe sanctuary for my boat but also eliminated the worry of her being left exposed to the elements on its moorings during what could be turbulent times. The club is an excellent association of keen and considerate members who will always help each other as well as everyone maintaining a watchful eye on each others' boats. Its impressive and hospitable clubhouse stands out proudly on the cliff top at Thurstaston overseeing the moorings two hundred yards away. The club also has its own 'moorings officer 'who maintains a pedantic check on each and every member's moorings with or without its boat all year round. I would certainly advocate any budding boat owner or sailing enthusiast who has aspirations of mooring their vessels in the area to consider joining our club of keen sailors, yachtsmen and yachtswomen.

Dee Sailing Club logo

Should the applicant be successful, becoming a member would reap the many advantages such membership can offer as well as its ongoing popular socialising events for members to enjoy. Members of the Dee Sailing Club to come from many walks of life and each are very friendly and willing to help each other and share whatever individual nautical skills each may have to offer. Although, (*at the time of writing this book*), due to circumstances beyond my control, my physical *boating* activities have now sadly ceased, nevertheless, I *still* enjoy my privileged membership, which I *strongly recommend* to other boating enthusiasts.

Chapter Twelve

A Pure Pedigree, Dee Estuary Born and Bred

After my nautical and lengthy honeymoon period with my Offshore Mirror diesel yacht cum fishing boat, I eventually moved into the 'First Division' of those who took sea fishing seriously by purchasing a real, purpose built sea fishing boat.

Although 'Block Skipper' (one) had given me many extremely happy trips out into the great blue yonder I decided to move on when I was given the opportunity to buy the recently converted West Kirby Sailing Club's rescue boat 'CAWDY'. This boat started life when it was built by the highly skilled and very reputable boat builder Sid Higgins at his West Kirby boat yard near to what was then the West Kirby Hotel (now the Moby Dick hotel). Sid's boats were much sought after by clients from far and wide, such was his respected reputation as builder of safe and reliable boats of all kinds. Sid built the thirty two foot long, clinker built boat with a nine foot six inch beam which went to the West Kirby Sailing club. She immediately assumed the role of the club's rescue boat and was named 'CAWDY'. After a period of commendable service in that role under the command and maintenance of the club's boatman and caretaker, the late Harry Jones (mentioned earlier) she was maintained to an extremely high standard.

Although Harry was the club's boatman, he was a very modest 'dark horse'. Harry was a former coxswain of the Hoylake lifeboat and whilst in that role he was awarded the RNLI Bronze medal for saving the lives of three people who were stranded on their yacht, the 'TRUGININI' in ferocious, stormy waters off the North Wales coast in the Dee estuary. As the result of his conscientious, dedicated and extremely valuable services to the North West and Lancashire fishing industries (as well as his dedication to the RNLI as a lifeboat crewman) Harry was also invested with a well deserved MBE. It was indeed an honour to have been included among Harry's extremely

The late Harry Jones MBE

wide circle of friends. Harry would never hesitate to help and assist anyone who was in any way in need of his many skills regarding boats, fishing and the sea. I am certainly grateful to have received his advice and assistance on many occasions.

During my seagoing fishing activities CAWDY was subsequently acquired by another former RNLI lifeboat crew member who is also a highly skilled and popular Hoylake boat builder, Allan Tolley (also previously mentioned). Alan's wizardry converted what was an open decked, club rescue vessel into an 'all singing, all dancing' sea angling boat. She was powered by a highly reliable and much sought after Lister 45 BHP Diesel inboard engine and her fuel tank held a substantial twenty five gallons, what more could I want? The end result of Alan's highly skilled transformation labours produced a sea fisherman's dream.

The vessel was magnificent and I couldn't resist the wonderful opportunity to acquire such a boat as this. True to his reputation for efficiency and the

The boat building genius Alan Tolley

interest of his clients, Alan accompanied me out to sea for a couple of familiarisation trips to ensure I became used to handling the boat and the various items of safety equipment on board. Alan's kind assistance and the new boat's handling 'tuition' was gratefully received and duly noted.

I renamed the 'new' boat BLOCK SKIPPER and her highly visible name was duly painted fore and aft of the vessel. Before the boat became 'fully operational' I would have the radio installed (call sign MQMY-8) together with its deck speakers. Other fittings would include a large aft facing headlight to accompany the already fitted navigation lights. For added protection from the elements to those on deck I would add a surrounding protective dodger. Inside the boat's wheelhouse I would add to these essential items a chart table and cooker (fed by a gas bottle out on deck) and seat. I would also store inside the wheelhouse lifejackets, oilskins, cups, dishes and kettle etc. I invented a 'Tide Clock' for display outside the wheelhouse for the information of all aboard, which was later manufactured in plastic and sold via the 'Lifeboat' magazine. Needless to say, I was delighted with the new Block Skipper and couldn't wait for her to become a fully fledged sea going fishing, shrimping and angling boat. The vessel was an enviable example of the innovative conversion skills of a true master of his craft, the highly skilled Alan Tolley of Hoylake.

At the conclusion of our 'see trials' the new boat would be taken on a two hour trip from Hoylake to its moorings at Thurstaston opposite the Dee Sailing Club. However, before this could be done the new boat was dramatically engaged in a 'rescue mission'!

A yacht had broken its moorings at Meols and drifted out of control for a mile along the coast. The heavy surf of a high tide started to crash the vessel against the sea wall at Moreton. With my pal and crewman Rob Slee and I immediately took the new Block Skipper down to the stricken vessel and I ventured into the surf as close as I could so that Rob could jump aboard

Author at Hoylake with the former Cawdy, now the new BLOCK SKIPPER (Prior to her being 'fitted out' ready for her new role)

the casualty and secure a towing line. This was no easy feat for Rob as the two vessels were bobbing up and down violently and not in unison. In no time, a small crowd gathered (which happened to included two of Rob's friends Brian Kelly and Barry Norman) to watch the seaborne drama. After a number of very 'hairy moments' when Rob was almost thrown into the waves, he eventually managed to succeed in securing the towing line to the casualty's bow. Once this was done, Rob precariously remained aboard the by now badly damaged boat as I slowly and carefully pulled the yacht out and away from the heavy surf with Rob clinging on for dear life. The boat was by now taking in water and starting to sink. With tender loving care and the reassuring, powerful throb of the Skipper's forty five horse power Lister Diesel engine we gently managed to tow the yacht to a more calm area where it was grabbed by Rob's two friends who followed us along the shoreline as the drama unfolded. The two bravely waded into the water, waist deep, and dragged the boat safely ashore out of harm's way. Finally, the exercise was successfully completed and the boat was eventually recovered and towed away for repair. During the whole of the operation, the Coastguard was kept informed by radio. This little drama was no doubt the 'christening' of my new *operational* ownership of (the second) Block Skipper!

After the furore died down, a few days later Block Skipper was taken to its new home inside the Dee estuary at Thurstaston to join the rest of the 'fleet' of local shrimp and fishing boats. My latest vessel became an instant hit with all who came aboard word spread among my former police colleagues as to the facility that was open to them should they wish to imbibe. The 'shiny' newly painted and named Skipper was an impressive sight as she sat bobbing about on her moorings opposite the Dee clubhouse. Not only did I intend to take my friends out on fishing trips, I would utilize her to my club's advantage during the annual Commodore's Cruise to the West Hoyle bank and other club's occasions as she was *more* than adequate to 'ferry' the club's equipment to and from the West Hoyle as well as conveying fellow members to the site to enjoy the day's Barbie and bar facilities and festivities. Block Skipper was a brilliant vessel for such occasions and I would always ensure she was available for my club for such events should she be needed.

After my familiarisation trips with Alan Tolley, *a man I hold in very deep esteem*, I soon became adept at her various attributes and my fishing trips out into Liverpool bay and the Dee Estuary commenced without delay!

Before such trips could take place however, I went ahead with having the various fittings and safety equipment all in place as a priority. Once this was done, the boat was then the epitome of absolute sea going safety for all aboard, nothing less was acceptable. I had learned *many* seagoing safety attributes and requirements from the likes of Dave Dodd, Alan Tolley, Harry Jones and the rest of the local fishermen and shrimpers for which I would be eternally grateful.

Rob Slee hoisting masthead flag, Author in wheelhouse (Note Deck speaker, Deck light and yellow plastic dodgers already in place)

All the work carried out to ensure all was 'correct' took a number of days and involved the kind efforts of a number of friends. Finally, when this was done, that was done, cables clipped, radio antenna fitted and protective dodger fitted to the deck rails the boat was all ready to 'rock 'n roll.' I would like to thank profusely, all those who kindly assisted in fitting the various items to the boat so that she became a very safe sea going vessel. To each and every pal who so kindly gave their time and effort, I would like to offer my deep and sincere gratitude to you all. Without your kind efforts, Block Skipper would not have become the fantastic boat she was.

Right from the start our trips out in the new Skipper went without a hitch. Before each trip, I would 'Book out' via radio to the Coastguard notifying them of my intended destination, how many (of each sex if applicable) were aboard, times of departure and return and I would insist from the very outset that each person aboard was either wearing or in possession of, a lifejacket. I would never take any shortcut or compromise the safety of all aboard, such was my compliance to the requirements of the rules of seagoing safety.

It was not uncommon for me and Tom (the Bosun) or Rob to take as many as six or eight anglers out for a day's fishing. There was more than adequate room for all to enjoy a relaxing day at sea. My passengers nearly always consisted of former or serving colleagues of Tom and me from either the police or fire services. Each time we would return with a decent catch of fish which would be shared around as some would sometimes return 'empty handed'. On one occasion our fishing party consisted of most of the senior officers from the Number One District Police Training Centre at Bruche (the Police Academy). No fees were ever charged as Tom or Rob and I would be going out for a day's fishing anyway.

I became inundated with requests from friends, relatives and former colleagues from my previous fire and police services for a day's fishing out in the new boat. I was more than happy to oblige and as a consequence, during the summer months I could always guarantee at least half a dozen keen anglers would accompany Tom or Rob and myself nearly every day. Block Skipper without doubt consumed a large part of my daily life out on the waters of the Irish Sea or the River Dee.

Author with senior officers from the Police Academy with their catch

My late wife Marje loved the bigger boat and enjoyed making mugs of tea in the wheelhouse to hand around to all aboard out on deck, my daughter Jo and son Ron also enjoyed the occasional trip out to sea but it was Marje who always liked to include a spot of fishing while we were out. They were extremely happy days and treasured memories to cherish. Another favourite place I liked to visit was across the River Dee on the Flintshire coast. I liked to pop over to see the once majestic ocean liner, the 'Duke of Lancaster'.

The liner started life as a steamer passenger ship that operated in European waters. However, it is now in a very sad state beached near Mostyn Docks. The ship, along with two other 'Dukes', was the last passenger only steamers which were built for British Railways. She was built at Harland and Wolff, Belfast in 1956 and designed to be both a ferry and a cruise ship. Sadly, as time went on such ships as the Duke were gradually replaced by car ferries. At one stage the Duke of Lancaster had her main deck rebuilt to accommodate vehicles via door at her stern. The ship then provided space for

The author and his late wife Marje en-route to the Duke of Lancaster

one thousand two hundred passengers and one hundred and five cars. The ship was finally laid up at Barrow in Furness in Cumbria.

After giving faithful service in her various ferry and cruising roles the Duke of Lancaster finally arrived at her final resting place in North Wales where it was intended she would become a 'Fun Ship'. From the start it appeared the Duke's owners were experiencing having difficulties with the local authority. The authority seemed to be in favour of the 'Fun Ship' project at first but they refused various planning applications and bar licensing applications. Eventually Magistrates issued a summons regarding the lack of fire sufficient escapes then a further application was made for a High Court injunction to close the ship on safety grounds. The owners finally closed the ship to business in 2004. Despite the vessel having large areas of its outer shell covered in rust the interior of the ship is still in good condition.

It is hoped one day, to transform the ship into a large, open air art gallery. The ship is slowly being covered with graffiti which has been described as bright and surreal? That is a matter of opinion! What a sad demise for such a once majestic maiden of the seas. I somehow had a fond liking for the ship

A painting of the gracious Duke of Lancaster in her glory days

The present tired and sad state of the Duke of Lancaster as she is today

and would sail across the Dee pay frequent visits to her (when I was not fishing). Many times I would drop anchor and fish near the Duke so that those on board who were interested in her could photograph the ship on learning of her sad history.

The beautiful, well known Hilbre Islands, a bird sanctuary, three miles off the West Kirby shoreline is a magnet for locals, tourists and ornithology enthusiasts alike. However, *extreme care* must be taken at all times when contemplating walking out to the islands. Looking out from west Kirby across the sands when the tide is out is very tempting. All appears to be safe enough to take a docile stroll out to the islands which deceptively look quite close. However, the very opposite is the case. Anyone intending to visit the islands MUST ensure it is entirely safe to do so. Sadly, some who have taken it for granted that a walk across the sands to the islands will present no problem, have indeed paid with their lives?

By all means, take the opportunity to visit the beautiful scenic islands and nature reserve on West Kirby's doorstep at the mouth of the Dee Estuary. The

Deceptively close looking Hilbre Islands

three islands consist of Little Eye, Middle Eye and Hilbre. All are designated as the Hilbre Islands Nature Reserve.

The safest route out to the islands is to walk from West Kirby *at low tide* taking the safest route from the slipway at the bottom of Dee Lane near to the boating lake. Walk towards the Little Eye, keeping it to your *right*. On arrival at Little Eye, pass beyond it keeping it on your right then swing inwards to pass the Middle Eye on your *Left*.

Between Middle Eye and Hilbre itself continue on and take the track over the rocks to the little tidal pool. Once off the rocks turn left towards the wide pathway and opening at the south end of Hilbre. Do NOT cross direct to the Hilbre Island under any circumstances and do NOT cross from Hoylake. Anyone visiting the islands MUST check the tide table AND the weather conditions. On leaving the island to return to West Kirby STRICTLY FOLLOW THE REVERSE ROUTE from the islands and allow at least 3 HOURS before high water to make it safely back to the mainland. Remember, NEVER take chances with weather and tide times. On one occasion I had occasion to rescue an adult male and two children who had inadvertently (and foolishly) been cut off by the incoming tide. Tom (the Bosun) and I took them aboard and transferred them to a dinghy from which they were all safely deposited back on the beach to safety. It doesn't leave much to the imagination to think what would have happened to the trio had we not been in the right place at the right time on that fateful (but their lucky) day.

The Skipper made another successful 'rescue' mission while we were three miles out fishing off the North Wales coast. The radio crackled into life and I heard a radio call for assistance from one of the local fishing boats (which I won't name) which had wrapped its nets around the propeller. As I was the nearest vessel to him I made haste out to the scene and was able to take him in tow. The Block Skipper's powerful Lister engine had no trouble towing the stricken fishing boat the eight miles back to the safety of its mooring at Thurstaston.

As well as somehow finding time for my ongoing scriptures, (I had become a resident columnist in a couple of magazines and newspapers and was also blessed with having a number of books successfully published), I decided once again to commit my latest Block Skipper to canvas. I painted

Block Skipper under way towing casualty back to its moorings

Author's latest painting in oils of Block Skipper fishing off Hilbre Island

Oil painting of author fishing aboard Block Skipper

two pictures of her in oils and had each framed. One is now adorning the walls of my home and the other I presented to the Coastguard service to hang in their Headquarters at Crosby on the outskirts of Liverpool. The latter painting (below) depicts Block Skipper fishing off Hilbre Island. Rob Slee is busy out on deck gutting and cleaning fish while the author can be seen in the wheelhouse at the helm.

Our continual outings in the 'Skipper' with my angling pals many times brought home a variety of fish for the 'pot'. Some of those caught included cod, garfish, and amazingly even a halibut succumbed to a large mackerel strip out near the Bar lightship on one occasion!

As I was fortunate to have landed the halibut to include amongst my list of catches, I will also include a couple of recipes to furnish more extremely tasty meals.

The tasty HALIBUT

First,

Garlic Halibut Fillets *(Serves two)*

Ingredients

Two halibut fillets

One teaspoon of olive oil

One clove of garlic, minced

Two teaspoons of lemon zest

Juice of half a lemon, divided

One tablespoon of chopped parsley

Salt and pepper to taste

Method

- Pre heat oven to 400F.
- Place halibut into a baking tray, skin side down and drizzle with oil.
- Top with the garlic, lemon zest, two tablespoons of lemon juice and chopped parsley then season with salt and pepper.
- Bake for twelve to fifteen minutes until the halibut flakes easily when tested with a fork.
- Drizzle with the remaining lemon juice and serve.

Also, you may like to try ...

Halibut with Snap Pea Salad

For this excellent gastronomic delight the following ingredients are needed.

One tablespoon of fresh lime juice
One tablespoon of grated fresh ginger
Two tablespoons of olive oil
Salt and black pepper
Twelve ounces of snap peas
One red onion, thinly sliced
Four six ounce pieces of halibut fillet
One lime, cut into wedges

Method

- Place into a large bowl, the lime juice, gingerone tablespoon of the oil and sprinkle with salt and pepper. Add the snap peas and onion the mix about to combine with a coating of the oil. Heat the remaining tablespoon of oil in a large non-stick skillet over medium high heat.
- Season the fish with salt and pepper and cook for three to five minutes on each side.
- Serve with the salad and lime wedges.
- Other fish caught are whiting, turbot but the majority of our catches were mainly plaice and other 'flatties'. Nevertheless, each fish caught ensured a most enjoyable day was had by all out on the waters of the Irish Sea and River Dee.
- Here are a couple of recipes for those who fancy a fantastic meal of Turbot. The first is a straight forward recipe to try with a fresh catch.
- After cleaning and gutting the fish, lightly score the skin around the base of the dorsal and ventral fins as this will make it easier to remove the skin once the fish is cooked.
- Place the fish into a baking tin and add 600 mls (one and a half pints) of water. Poach the fish in a pre heated oven at 230C for twenty minutes then remove the dark top skin.

- Reduce the cooking water to just two tablespoons. Make a mixture of melted butter with chopped parsley, bay, chives and thyme and pour over the fish. Carefully remove the flesh from the bones with a spatula, lift the flesh away from the bone to a plate. Remove the spine and serve the rest of the flesh. To finish off such a splendid meal add a tomato salad and new potatoes to serve, I guarantee a most enjoyable meal will be well worth the effort.

Another Turbot delight is Broiled Garlic Turbot Fillets

Ingredients

Two turbot fillets
Two teaspoons of olive oil
Two tablespoons of lemon juice
Two garlic cloves, crushed
A pinch of oregano and paprika

Method

- Lay the fillets side by side in a lightly oiled platter. Mix together the oil, lemon juice, oregano and garlic and brush onto the fish. Broil the turbot fillets in oven or over barbecue for six to eight minutes, brushing fish with juices every two minutes.

Broiled garlic Turbot

I mentioned having also caught one or two Garfish on occasions. Such occasions were *very* much appreciated as this fish was certainly a treat to take home for ultimate consumption. The fish is not unlike an eel at first sight being blue green in colour with silver sides but it differs by having a long beak like a bird. Garvin are often found near or among shoals of mackerel but are actually a relative of the flying fish and can sometimes be seen leaping from the water to give an impressionable display of aerial somersaults above the waves. However, when bringing the fish aboard beware, as care must be taken when handling and removing the hook as the 'beak' contains rows of razor sharp teeth which are capable of inflicting a nasty wound.

The main attribute of the splendid Garfish is its unique and extremely tasty flavour which provides for many various dishes. I would certainly be failing my gastronomic scriptures if I didn't include a couple of *very* tasty recipes to satisfy the appetite of those who enjoy an unusual variety sea cuisine. Hare is but a small selection.

Steamed Garfish Salad *(Serves two)*

Ingredients

One Garfish, filleted
One large tomato
One large onion
Shredded, pickled cucumber
3 cm (two inches) of root ginger, half sliced and half shredded
Two teaspoons of soya sauce
One tablespoon of sesame oil
Spring onions
Shallots
Salt and Pepper

Method

- Fill base of a steamer with water and bring to the boil.
- Descale and wash the fish then rub with salt and pepper. Make deep cuts in the fish meat and insert the small slices of ginger.
- Arrange slices of the onion on a soup plate and lay the fish on top.

The versatile (and very tasty) Garfish

A very tempting Garfish salad

- Top the fish with pickled cucumber, sliced tomatoes and shredded ginger then sprinkle the soya sauce over.
- Steam for eight minutes until the fish turns white and begins to flake.
- Heat up the oils in a small pan and fry some shallots. Pour the sizzling oil over the fish and top with chopped spring onions.
- Serve with boiled rice and then spoon over the sauce gathered at the bottom of the fish. I doubt if there can be a better tasting salad than this?

If you are lucky enough to catch *a couple* of garfish, these will furnish a quick, easy and equally delightful meal which takes only minutes to prepare.

Ingredients

Two Garfish
Two tablespoons of crushed garlic
Fresh Olive oil
Half a cup of chopped parsley
Salt

Method

- Soak the garfish with the garlic in the olive oil for TWO HOURS
- Then place under a very hot grill with a small amount of olive oil and quickly char. Remove and sprinkle with chopped parsley and season with salt. Yet *another* gastronomic little gem to savour!

Skipper en-route to her winter moorings at Heswall

At the end of each season it was always the time for Block Skipper to have to leave her moorings at Thurstaston. I would take her three mile trip further up river to the sanctuary of her winter moorings at 'Hughie's' (the late Hughie Higgins) boatyard at Lower Heswall.

There, whatever the weather threw at her during the winter months I could rest in the knowledge that the boat would be safe and secure. Once in position and safely moored amongst the rest of the boats who vacated Thurstaston with me for the winter, I would be kindly assisted by Skippers' numerous anglers and long standing friends who would help me to undertake the various and essential maintenance work that is necessary to ensure that a boat's continual life of seaworthiness is never demeaned. Such work includes scraping, removing the season's barnacles, sealing any leaks found, painting, varnishing and engine inspection, maintenance and overhaul (if necessary). These very important meticulous tasks and annual procedures are the absolute norm for those of us who own seagoing boats of any size, large or small.

Author's pal and fellow fisherman Cliff Langley helps with winter maintenance (yellow dodger removed and rails scraped and repainted)

The saying, 'Many hands make light work' was always true in the case of the popular Block Skipper. I was never short of enthusiastic helpers who were more than willing to spend time working on the boat, even during bad weather if it was essential to do so. I remain profusely grateful to each and every one of them. Some even travelled over to Heswall from Liverpool and its outskirts. That is why I would never dream of accepting any offer from them towards fuel costs during our fishing trips. My refusals were reciprocal to express my profuse gratitude to them all for their kind assistance when I needed help with work on the boat. This same privilege was always the sort of unique bond I also experienced amongst the local fishermen and shrimpers I mixed with.

Eventually, after her winter's 'rest', overhaul and a good spruce up, the clean and sparkling Skipper is taken back to her usual place back by the sailing club.

Cliff puts final touches to newly painted Skipper ready for new season

Chapter Thirteen

Fishing Waters Near and Far

On one of Skipper's first trips to start a new summer season was a combined checkout trip which would include a spot of fishing. This time however, we had unusual, but delightful canine company in the shape of Rob's beautiful dog 'Jess', a blonde Labrador. Although the trip was more of a pre season trip out to check all was well, Rob and I nevertheless enjoyed a day's fishing out at the Mersey Bar. Although my day brought nothing special aboard, my lucky pal Rob managed to hook a large cod which amused Jess no end as she watched fascinated as it jumped and wriggled about noisily in the large skerries fish box.

Rob and 'Jess' about to come aboard

Rob couldn't wait to get his catch home so that his charming wife Sheila, a brilliant chef and seafood connoisseur, would transform the aquatic delight into the evening's dinner.
His favourite cod dish would be that of ***Baked Cod Fillets in Chorizo***.

Ingredients

Two cod fillets
Two tablespoons of olive oil
Four ounces of chorizo (cured sausage) thinly sliced
One pond of potatoes, sliced a quarter of an inch thick
Two leeks, (the white and green parts) cut into thin half moons
A quarter of a teaspoon of crushed saffron threads
Salt and black pepper
A quarter of a cup of fresh parsley roughly chopped

Method

- Heat oven to 400F.
- Heat one tablespoon of the oil in a large ovenproof skillet over medium heat.
- Add the sausage and cook for two or three minutes, tossing occasionally until browned.
- Add the potatoes and cook for ten minutes, stirring occasionally. Add the leeks, saffron, half a cup of water, pepper and half a teaspoon of salt then bring to the boil.
- Season the cod with salt and pepper and place on top of the potatoes then drizzle with the remaining tablespoon of oil.
- Transfer the skillet to the oven and bake for fifteen to twenty minutes.
- Sprinkle with the parsley before serving.

My day's 'tally' was a 'flattie', a decent sized fluke and a small plaice which I put back into the water to live and fight another day. An added treat was the regular sightings of the seals frolicking about on the banks of the West Hoyle as we passed by into the river. Some were so inquisitive they were almost tame as their heads bobbed out of the water near the boat.

Block Skipper alongside inquisitive seals playing on the West Hoyle bank

When Rob was not out in Skipper he was also a keen shrimp fisherman and was often off across the sands and into the shallows pushing his net for the delightful crustaceans.

I too was always keen to reap shrimps and cockles but as time went on, the local shores were becoming saturated with literally hordes of people from here, there and everywhere taking cockles until such time the stocks started to become depleted. Indeed, such was the case in Cumbria, the authorities became so concerned, the police introduced (honestly!) a 'Cockles' Officer!

As our shores became 'crowded' with cockle pickers who were hell bent on making a lucrative living out of them, it became clear that *something* would eventually 'give'?

As it happened, a terrible tragedy would come about that would completely pale the concern for the diminishing cockle population into insignificance. A number of unsupervised and *totally* inexperienced cockle pickers ventured

The newly introduced 'Cockles' officer

out over the unfamiliar (to them) sands of Morecambe Bay with their rakes, riddles and sacks hoping to make lots of money from their potential haul. Sadly, a lot of those poor, ignorant pickers (the majority of them foreigners) were totally oblivious to the times and depth of the tides and where and where not to make their way over parts that were 'quick sands'. The inevitable result was a catastrophic tragedy and many were marooned by an incoming tide and sadly, *twenty one* of them were to perish and drown before a rescue could be safely launched.

Due to such a tragedy occurring plus the already widely voiced concern over the dwindling beds themselves, one Police force decided to do something about ensuring our shorelines were to be safely monitored. As a consequence, Cumbria Police appointed an officer to work with those involved and affected by the cockling industry. Cumbria Police's new cockling officer thus began work alongside other organisations to improve safety to those working out

ESTABLISHED 1864

Police News

THE NATIONAL INDEPENDENT NEWSPAPER FOR THE POLICE SERVICE

Issue 04 www.police-news.co.uk May 2010

What next in the search for Madeleine?

by Staff Reporter

THREE years since the launch of the Portuguese police investigation into the disappearance of Madeleine McCann, from the family's holiday apartment in Praia da Luz on the Algarve, the case remains one of the most high profile unsolved international police investigations.

Maddie vanished on the evening of 3 May 2007, days before her fourth birthday and her parents Kate and Gerry McCann, from Rothley in Leicestershire, are obviously as committed as ever in

we have developed a number of significant lines of enquiry and continue to receive information from the public.

"As a small team we have to be very focused, but what we lose on size we more than make up for in terms of flexibility and practical experience."

And Leicestershire Police continues to co-ordinate work on any leads and follow up as necessary. This includes passing information to the Portuguese authorities, who are in the lead on this case, as appropriate.

Leicester Constabulary said anyone with information

The former national Police newspaper, host of author's column

Cumbria Police 'Cockle' Officers

'Cockle officer on Parade'

on the cockle beds and to also reduce disruption by noise and vehicle parking near to residential areas. At that time I was a resident columnist in the former national newspaper 'Police News' and I wrote an illustrated, two page feature on this great idea after visiting the area with my paper's editor Shirley Chisnall. There, I interviewed Inspector Vernon his subordinate constable regarding the creation of the new, important post. Since the tragedy there had been tensions over access to the Morecambe Bay beds. Inspector Vernon informed me that although the health and safety of those out cockling on the sands isn't directly a police responsibility, the police, intended to contribute fully to the work of other agencies to improve the cocklers' safety as well as to reduce the risk of potential disorder.

Thankfully, no such tragedy has occurred to the shorelines of Wirral but, I do consider that perhaps a similar police involvement may well be beneficial to create and maintain similar assurances of safety and discipline to such activity as it is now common knowledge that the 'invasion' of cocklers to the beaches of Hoylake, West Kirby and the Dee estuary has certainly caused rise for concern at the inevitable depletion of cockle beds that has ensued. The strict introduction of licences and 'prohibited cockling' areas *has* improved the situation but it may be a long time before the area is back to anywhere near to how it once was?

My faithful and reliable Block Skipper continued to furnish our trips out to fish the waters of the Irish Sea and many fish continued to be caught to satisfy the numerous anglers who graced her decks.

Many trips were undertaken at night either to fish or, to travel to various destinations way down the North Wales coast. As previously mentioned, my favourite place to visit was the Isle of Anglesey (or 'Ynys Mon' in welsh). Our nocturnal trips were nearly always undertaken just by myself and Rob Slee or Tom 'the Bosun' Oram, my two eager and enthusiastic fishermen crew. On *very* rare occasions we did have a keen serving or former service colleague who insisted on joining us for a few hours of nocturnal fishing. Night or day, we never returned empty handed, there was always someone who had caught something!

Our night fishing trips out off the North Wales coast were always enjoyable and we listened to the other vessels' radio traffic or engaged in

Author about to set off out on overnight fishing trip

conversation with some of the local fishing boats as we sat bobbing about at anchor fishing the dark depths. I always had the kettle simmering on the hob to furnish an ongoing demand for continual mugs of tea as I sat with my feet up in the wheelhouse, my fishing rod propped up close at hand ready to 'haul in' should I get a knock.

Each year the new season would start all over again and Rob, Tom and me would be busy out and about trawling for shrimps or hosting a couple of anglers. Rob Slee and I would also be active on the shore gathering cockles or wading in the shallows with our shrimp nets. Another successful method of ensuring a large catch was to spread a trammel net across the channel then Rob and I would take to a dinghy yards downstream of the incoming tide then plunge the oars into the water making a loud noise and splash. This would send the fish darting into the nets. The same procedure would be repeated yards upstream of the ebbing tide to net more fish. When the water ran off we would then fill our sack with fish, dismantle the net then walk

Night drifter. 'Skipper' fishing at night

ashore, usually with a *very* full sack of fish, consisting mainly of flukes, dabs and flounders with the bonus of the occasional plaice.

Our hobby, because it was no more than that, was insatiable. Rob had amazed me by retaining one or two weever fish from his push net which he had later cooked and consumed, informing that they were 'quite tasty'! Mmmmm, Not for me I'm afraid.

As always the Block Skipper behaved impeccably and her Lister engine never misbehaved in any way whatsoever. I continued to visit our usual fishing specks and very occasionally ventured round the top of the peninsular into the then murky waters of the busy river Mersey. One such trip took Tom and me down as far as Liverpool Pier head. The trip was just a cruise and I took some photographs of various boats I passed during the day's outing.

Our return trip took us back past New Brighton and along past Moreton and Hoylake to Hilbre Island before heading back to our moorings at Thustaston.

Such trips were always most enjoyable and were a nautical adventure as we ventured into 'foreign' waters.

The former well known ferry Royal Iris at Liverpool Pier head

The abandoned Royal Iris languishes on the River Thames

Sadly, the immensely popular Royal Iris was to eventually succumb to the dreaded 'cutbacks' syndrome that now prevails to blight our heritage. Her once graceful lines no longer enhance the Mersey scenery as she plied up and down the river between Liverpool and Wirral. The beautiful vessel now languishes on the banks of the River Thames in London, her future uncertain as she lies abandoned and rusting away pictured below at the start of 2017.

It is doubtful if the once beautiful Royal Iris, a true nautical princess, will ever be seen on the Mersey again?

Although all was going well for a while I was however, continuing to experience problems with my legs, both of which had sustained serious injury when I had been deliberately run down whilst on police duty. I had already undergone major surgery during which time I had three knee replacement operations on my left leg. My right leg too had been badly damaged. Such injuries brought about the premature end to my career as a police officer. My right leg had become so bad it had become necessary to amputate the limb high above the knee. This immediately put paid to my boating and fishing activities at a stroke.

Due to these tragic developments my cherished Block Skipper and I had to reluctantly part company I sadly had to sell her, lock, stock and barrel. After my latest major operation, prosthesis was attempted but this proved unsuccessful and I began a new life on the seat of my pants in a wheelchair.

As if this unenviable scenario that had been brought about due to an act of gratuitous violence by a piece of low life scum was not enough, when I needed her most, my beloved wife of forty years, Marjorie succumbed to cancer. I was totally shattered and devastated. After suffering such an inconsolable loss it took some time for me to get my wrecked life back into some semblance of order. I was wandering about in a mental wilderness.

Fortunately, with the help of my 'children', daughter Jo and son Ron I slowly started to pick up the pieces. The three of us also had the additional help of a loyal family friend of long standing Mrs Christine Lucas. Chris had always been at hand if or when she could assist in any way during Marje's unexpected terminal illness. With the unrelenting help of such a dynamic trio I decided on a totally different way of life.

I became an ardent and *obsessive* fundraiser to seek much needed cash to assist seeking a cure, treatment and valuable research since Marje's premature demise. My obsessive devotion to this cause put absolutely *everything* on the 'back boiler' during my deep, heartbroken grief. My deeply dedicated and sincere enthusiasm knew no bounds and my (many times eccentric) fundraising efforts eventually began to raise considerable amounts of money to the coffers of the Clatterbridge (Cancer) Hospital at Bebington, Wirral where every effort had been made to save my beloved wife. Clatterbridge is a *major* Cancer research hospital which treats patients from near and (very) far.

As well as performing many physically demanding events to raise and generate funds, I also gave illustrated addresses to many organisations and associations such as Rotary, Round Table, Lions, Masonic lodges as well as to local women's' guilds, clubs, scouts, and cadets etc. Eventually my fundraising curriculum started to take me to foreign places to assist those in need in less fortunate and needier countries than here in the U.K. My efforts abroad took me first to the distant Falkland Islands. I was surprised to learn that Clatterbridge Hospital had even treated patients from those far away islands down in the South Atlantic. I am proud to say that my fundraising efforts on the islands were a resounding success.

My hosts down there were fantastic. I made many friends during my stay, friendships that remain to this day.

Never one to miss an opportunity, although the waters were very cold, I could not resist the lure of the sea and I borrowed a sturdy fishing rod and propelled my trusty 47lb NHS issue wheelchair with its little front casters, out into the chilly waters of the South Atlantic.

My first attempt at sea fishing since becoming a member of the 'Chairbourne Infantry' was a success and I caught a large mullet. My first amazed (and amused) hostess cooked and served us all a fabulous fish dinner that evening.

Before I returned home to Great Britain, I was given the honour and privilege of being formally invited by His Excellency the Governor of the

Author with his Falklands catch

Falkland Islands, Mr Donald Lamont and his charming wife Lynda to dinner in the islands' capital Stanley at Government House.

During a most enjoyable dinner His Excellency had somehow become aware of my 'fishing trip' and was amused at my most unusual method of entering the chilly waters to 'catch my supper' as he put it. Although my Falklands fishing trip was successful and I managed to hook a fish, I must

His Excellency the Governor of the Falkland Islands

admit, it was certainly an unorthodox and most unusual form of (wheelchair) sea angling I had ever undertaken.

Here is the mouth watering recipe my Falkland hostess prepared.

Baked Mullet (The Falklands Way)

Ingredients

One (my) Mullet
Butter
Parsley sprigs
Onion, thinly sliced
Salt and pepper
White wine

Method

- Gut and skin the fish and remove its head.
- Butter a roasting tin that will take the fish. Spread three or four sprigs of parsley, some sliced onion then sprinkle some salt and pepper in the tray. Place the fish into the tray and lay more sliced onion on top. Add a little more salt and pepper, pour a quarter of a pint of white wine over all, dot with more butter and cover tightly with foil. Bake in a moderate oven allowing twenty minutes per pound.
- Serve with mashed, new or plain boiled potatoes, peas or broccoli.

You don't *have* to go all the way down to the islands to enjoy such a brilliant fish dinner, just go out and catch a mullet! and then emulate my Falkland hostess's culinary skills. I can assure you, she won't mind, her tasty cuisine will not fail to impress those who take advantage of such a delightful (Falklands) meal.

During our long return flight to RAF Brize Norton, Matron and I had the privilege of a week long stay on the beautiful, tropical Ascension Island. This was our halfway refuelling stop on the long, eight thousand mile return trip to the UK. During our stay I gave an illustrated talk to raise funds for the island's scouts and guides. The island is truly a tropical paradise and our hosts were mainly Saint Helenians (or Saints as they are *officially* referred as).

Each night during our stay I would wheel to the pier and fish with an improvised hand line by dropping my hook down to the waters below. It was amazing, fish of all species gathered under or around the pier in abundance, day and night. Matron also enjoyed each night fishing from the pier and during our week long stay, between us we caught a number of Blackjacks and Tuna which we duly shared with our kind and hospitable hosts.

Back home, I resumed my fund raising role by various events and talks. Being blessed with my loyal pal Rob, I was supplied with copious supplies of cockles or razor fish or the added pleasure of shrimps whenever he ventured into the shallows with his push net.

On a couple of occasions I managed to accompany Rob out over the hard sand in my chair (with a struggle) to gather a few cockles but due to the physically demanding effort it took to do so I decided that this was not a viable proposition!

Although I missed being out fishing, especially in Block Skipper, my fundraising engagements diary started to fill considerably. I was receiving

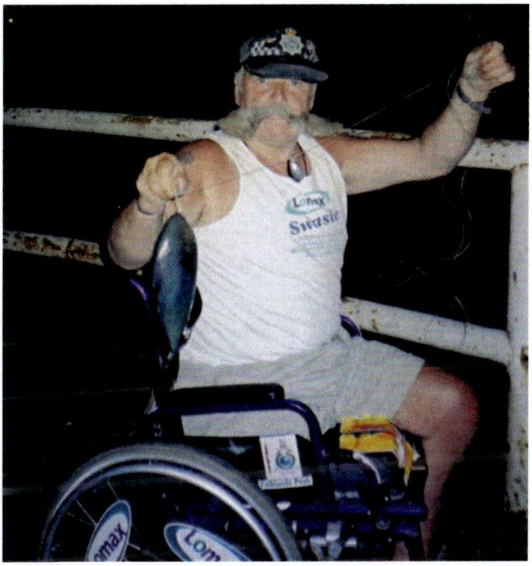

Author lands Ascension Blackjack

requests and bookings to give talks about my 'unusual' events to generate much needed funds for my charities' coffers. By now I was collecting for other worthy causes as well as for my number one cancer charity. As I needed transport to the various venues, Christine began to adopt the role of chauffeur when her duties as a store detective allowed. Consequently, my engagements would normally have to coincide with her off duty periods. As Chris was always at hand to be may carer and look after me she soon became affectionately known as 'Matron'. As a lot of my fundraising exploits were not the *normal* events one would carry out in a wheelchair such as ascending lighthouses, Blackpool Tower and pushing over to Hilbre Island, my efforts were deemed by many as eccentric! However, the unbelievers amongst them donated generously when I successfully completed such endeavours much to their amazement. Such eccentric events were my intention as everything I set out to do would always be a 'First'. As well as conveying me and my chair to where-ever I was to complete a fundraising 'event' Matron now became my personal 'David Bailey' and would photograph each and every event to enable my talks to be illustrated. This ensured the authenticity of whatever 'unbelievable' or impossible endeavour I had completed. My illustrated talks soon became the subject of discussion among the 'after dinner' circuit. As a result, my engagements diary filled to capacity. Matron's pictures had the absolute desired effect. My telephone constantly rang requesting me to give my talks to large and small associations and clubs. I even gave my illustrated verbal renditions to Tranmere Rovers and Liverpool football clubs, each of who gave generously to my charity bucket.

I became aware of a hospital which would benefit considerably by aid to secure various items of much needed equipment. The hospital was on the remote, beautiful tropical of Saint Helena, in the middle of nowhere in the vast expanses of the ocean. On learning of their dire needs, Matron and I packed our cased and set off on our lengthy trip to the island. Saint Helena boasted the notorious 'Jacob's Ladder, a nine hundred feet high set of seven hundred steps at forty five degrees to the top of a mountain out of Jamestown, the island's capital. I decided that taking my chair to the top of the structure would be certain to arouse the interest of the islanders and contacted the

Tranmere Rovers football club, Prenton, Birkenhead

Liverpool Football Club, Anfield, Liverpool

The awesome and infamous 900 ft, 700 steps of Jacob's ladder

Saint Helena authorities. They were delighted at the thought of someone taking the trouble to assist their hospital.

Chris and I travelled down to the island at our own expense. This involved flying from RAF Brize Norton to Ascension Island from where we would continue by a three day boat journey aboard the RMS ST. Helena. On our eventual arrival at the island, the sight of the 'Ladder', which could be clearly seen from the ship as we approached, was truly an awesome structure.

Matron and I enjoyed the extremely warm hospitality of our Saint Helena hosts (Saints as they were known by) for the few days we were on the island.

Amazingly, I successfully completed the ascent to the top of the ladder where I rested and enjoyed a cool, refreshing drink before returning to the ground on my long decent. Going down was a little more hazardous as my hands were slippy with sweat as I held onto the rails on my way down as my chair and I dropped down step by step. The whole island's residents were there to meet me on my return down to the base of the ladder in Jamestown. The whole venture was a total success and a lot of money was raised for the hospital. Matron and I were invited to go out each day for a couple days to

Matron makes sure all is photographed to furnish author's talks

Filling the decks

The highly skilled art of 'Hooking' Tuna

fish for yellow fin Tuna fishing on the fishing boat '*Helena Dorothy*' by its friendly skipper and owner named 'Darka'. I was intrigued to see how the boat fishermen caught the large, heavy fish.

They were literally hooked out of the water by a barbless hook, minus bait, on the tip of a long rod. The large, heavy fish were pulled out of the water and thrown up and over the fishermen's heads to crash onto the deck behind them, sending sprays of blood splattering everywhere as they landed. Although it looked easy, the operation was without doubt one which would obviously need a lot of practice and skill to successfully perform.

Just for the record, here's a recipe from my island hosts.

Grilled Yellowfin Tuna with Marinade

Ingredients

Four large Yellow fin Tuna steaks
Half a cup of vegetable oil
A third of a cup of soy sauce
A quarter of a cup of fresh lemon juice
Tow teaspoons of Dijon mustard
One teaspoon of grated lemon peel
One clove of garlic, crushed
Four wedges of lemon to garnish

Method

- Prick the steaks all over with a fork then place them into a shallow dish.
- Whisk the oil, soy sauce, lemon juice, Dijon mustard, lemon peel and garlic together in a bowl then pour over the steaks. Cover dish with Clingfilm and refrigerate for one to three hours.
- Pre heat grill to medium heat. Remove tuna from the marinade and shake excess moisture from the steaks. Pour the marinade into a small pan and bring to the boil. Reduce heat to medium low and simmer for ten minutes. Cook the tuna on the pre heated grill, basting with the boiled marinade until cooked through (about five or six minutes) each side then serve with the lemon wedges.

FANTASTIC ... I've tried it!

Before our return journey home, after a lot of cash had been donated by the islanders and their government leaders Chris and I were taken to meet the Matron, doctors, nurses and patients at the Jamestown Hospital. What an honour and privilege such a visit was. As well as making notes of various important I *may* be able to obtain from various medical sources in the UK, I also noted with interest various requests I received from doctors and staff for a number of items we here in the UK might consider to be 'small' or even

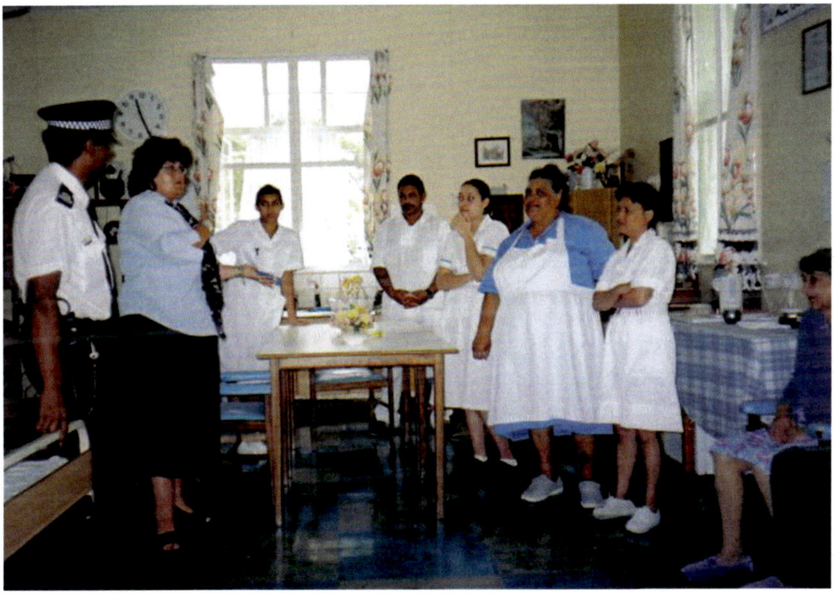

Staff and patients meet Chris, the other 'Matron' at Jamestown Hospital

irrelevant items we take for granted, but down on Saint Helena were near enough unobtainable. I promised that I would see what I could do to assist them on such matters.

Sadly it was time to leave the beautiful tropical paradise of Saint Helena Island and after bidding our charming and most hospitable hosts goodbye Chris and I returned home to Great Britain.

Once I returned back home to 'Blighty' I set about seeking various medical items that the Jamestown hospital was in dire need of. I managed to 'acquire' three new very expensive orthopaedic beds for the price of two. I was also able to beg a number of various items from a couple of hospitals so that all in all, I was able to have shipped nearly £25.000 worth of much needed medical equipment down to the Jamestown hospital on Saint Helena, (free of charge) courtesy of the extremely kind and benevolent Andrew Weir Shipping Company.

Back at author's home, Medical supplies being loaded for shipment (medical equipment kindly donated or 'acquired' leaving for the Saint Helena hospital)

Further charity fund raising events took me to various parts of the globe where fishing either was not, or could not be, on the agenda. Other foreign venues however did offer the opportunity to do some sea fishing when 'off duty' periods presented an opportunity.

During a 280 mile charity push along Western Australia's coastline from Augusta to Perth, I managed to get the opportunity to push my chair across the reasonably hard sand of the beach and into the sea at the sunny little resort of Rockingham. Once into the refreshingly cool waters I pushed until I was deep enough to roll out of the chair for a cool and pleasant 'dip'. After a most welcome cooling respite from my long, hot and physically demanding daily toil I was also able to relax during (a fruitless) two hours of beach angling. Three days later, after my swim and fishing break, I was mortified when I was informed that a youth had been taken by a shark and fatally injured at the very same spot where I had frolicked among the cooling waters. To make matters worse, I was also warned as to the ever present dangers of small jellyfish that abounded in the waters along the coastal route I was taking whose tentacle stings could easily kill a human being. Enough said, after that, *No more* relaxing dips in the seas off Australia.

However, I am proud to say that my long distance charity push did however manage to raise a substantial sum of money for the charity 'CANTEEN' (CANcer among TEENagers) which is an extremely worthy cause down under and the Police Welfare Fund.

Numerous other foreign fundraising jaunts continued as I maintain what is a different lifestyle to that I once enjoyed. Sadly, the life on the shore and venturing out onto and wading into, the waters around the Wirral shores fishing for shrimps, cockling and days out fishing the Dee estuary in Block Skipper are no more having been put paid to , thanks to my worthless assailant.

Thankfully, I do maintain a high standard of fitness and I push my castered, heavyweight little 'tank' around the locality of my home and the shoreline I once ventured over for cockles, razor fish and shrimps in days gone by. Nevertheless, I am still blessed with the privilege of maintaining my long standing friendships with those of the boating and shrimping fraternity who are still actively engaged in their 'profession', although their numbers have now dwindled and there are not the number of shrimp and fishing boats on the moorings there once were. I still enjoy visiting the lifeboat station at Hoylake to see my pals and the boat's crew who religiously maintain their vigil to ensure the safety of all who venture out onto the sometimes dangerous and unforgiving waters of our coastline.

The present lifeboat based at the new purpose built lifeboat station on the promenade at Hoylake is the brilliant all weather, all purpose, self righting RNLI vessel, the EDMUND HAWTHORN MICKLEWOOD, whose extremely able and worthy, highly professional coxswain, Andy Dodd is none other than the son of my pal David, himself a former Hoylake lifeboat coxswain who very kindly wrote the complimentary foreword to this book.

In conclusion, I hope this book is in some way an informative and educational read for those to learn of the dangers, pitfalls and also culinary advantages that abound on our foreshores and in our coastal waters. I would also like to thank profusely all those who assisted me by providing information for my pages. Although there are far too many to name I *would* like to extend my sincere best wishes to all of the fishing and shrimping fraternity whose friendship I have enjoyed over the years. A couple of those who stand out are Alan Tolley, Dave and Andy Dodd, Bobby Beech, the late Mick Ackroyd, the late Harry Jones MBE and many more whose priceless knowledge I benefitted from during my own most enjoyable 'nautical' and 'scavenging' days on the shore.

A striking picture of Hoylake Lifeboat passing Hilbre Island (photo courtesy of Nicholas Leach)

Andy Dodd, Coxswain of Hoylake Lifeboat
'EDMUND HAWTHORN MICKLEWOOD'
(photo by courtesy of Nicholas Leach)

Dedication

I would like to dedicate this book to all those exceptionally brave and dedicated men and women who crew our lifeboats in all weathers and conditions to save the lives of others. They unhesitatingly continue to venture out onto our sometimes turbulent and unforgiving waters.

Their true dedication and selfless courage knows no bounds and many of those have paid the ultimate price having given their lives during operations when they put to sea, day and night in all weathers and tempestuous conditions. Such brave volunteers of the RNLI lifeboat crews are worthily represented by one of a long listed Hoylake RNLI family, Coxswain Andrew Dodd, illustrated above whose father too served as a lifeboat coxswain at Hoylake.

I am *immensely* proud to be a Governor of the RNLI and equally proud to have the honour and privilege of being included among the circle of friends of such heroes.

Thank you and God bless each and every one of you.

Swasie Turner MBE

The author